VICTORIAN PAINTING

VICTORIAN PAINTING
in Oils and Watercolours

Christopher Wood

Antique Collectors' Club

British Library Cataloguing-in-Publication Data
A Catalogue record for this book is available from the British Library

Frontispiece. **ELEANOR FORTESCUE-BRICKDALE.** 'They toil not neither do they spin'

Printed in England on Consort Royal Art paper from Donside Mills, Aberdeen, by
Antique Collectors' Club Ltd., 5 Church Street, Woodbridge, Suffolk IP12 1DS

Contents

Colour Plate 1. **GEORGE CLAUSEN.** Harvest — Tying the Sheaves

Victorian Oil Paintings

Introduction

The nineteenth century was England's golden age, and it was also the golden age of English art. How else can one describe the century which produced Constable, Turner, John Martin, Landseer, Rossetti, Millais, Holman Hunt, Burne-Jones, Leighton, Albert Joseph Moore, G.F. Watts and Whistler? All of these artists lived in the reign of Queen Victoria, with the exception of Constable, who died in the year of the Queen's accession. Victoria's reign saw England's imperial, political, naval and mercantile power reach its apogee, and there can be no doubt that this produced a brilliant flowering of the arts, just as it had in Holland in the seventeenth century and France in the eighteenth. The first volume of this dictionary contains over 11,000 entries, which in itself underlines what a hugely prolific period it was. Inevitably, many of these names are extremely minor figures, or mediocrities, but there are also a great number of highly talented and accomplished artists, both male and female, as a glance through the illustrations in this volume will show. There were also a few artists of genius, and a great many individualists, such as Richard Dadd or John Atkinson Grimshaw (Colour Plate 2), whose work cannot easily be fitted into any category.

The strength and individuality of the British School was recognised, not only by Ruskin and the English critics, but by foreign writers as well. Both Baudelaire and Henry James wrote about English art, and histories of English nineteenth century art were written by both French and German writers. Moreover, many foreign artists settled in England, including Herkomer, Alma-Tadema, Tissot, Whistler and Sargent. For much of the twentieth century, the English neglected and despised the art of the nineteenth, but now a complete reassessment has taken place. At last it is possible to see the nineteenth century as part of the overall history of English art. The Victorian age is not only an integral part of our culture, but one of the most glorious chapters of its history.

The central institution of the Victorian art world was the Royal Academy. Founded in the eighteenth century, it attained its highest levels of power and prestige in the nineteenth, levels it has never recovered since. The opening of the Royal Academy Summer Exhibition was the beginning of the London Season, and a highly fashionable event. The levels of attendance were higher than at any time before or since, reaching a peak during the reign of Frederic Leighton, the most successful of all Academy Presidents. Just before his death, he was created Lord Leighton, the only English artist ever to have been raised to the peerage. Many other artists were awarded knighthoods, and Millais was the first to be made a baronet. The whole status of artists was raised to new heights during the nineteenth century, and an artist could be considered as a respectable, professional member of society, on a par with any other successful businessman. The letters RA after a name really could confer both respectability, and wealth. Few societies can have rewarded their artists so lavishly. Many Victorian artists became rich men; several died millionaires. Millais boasted, at the height of his fame, that he earned £30,000 a year, a huge income by today's standards. Many artists, including Millais, built enormous houses and studios; the favourite architect was Norman Shaw. Several of these houses can still be seen in Holland Park and Hampstead. Leighton House survives as a museum, and shows in what style a successful Victorian artist could live.

Throughout the nineteenth century, there were many challenges to the Royal Academy's monopoly. The Grosvenor Gallery, the New English Art Club, and the New Gallery were all intended as rival alternatives to the Academy. Although successful, they never succeeded in weakening the Academy's position. Many artists kept a foot in both camps by exhibiting at the Academy as well as at other galleries. The watercolourists had their own societies, and minor galleries also proliferated, such as the Royal Society of British Artists, the British Institution, the Dudley Gallery, the Royal Portrait Society, the Pastel Society, and the Society of Women Artists. Almost every Victorian artist could achieve some letters after his name. Artists' groups and colonies proliferated, as they did all over Europe in the nineteenth century. The Clique, the Pre-Raphaelite Brotherhood, the St. John's Wood Clique, the Cranbrook Colony and the Newlyn School are among the best known. Some of these groups may have started life as rebels against the Academy; most of their members ended up joining it. But it was by no means essential to belong to the RA; Holman Hunt, Burne-Jones, and John Linnell pursued successful careers outside the Academy, although Burne-Jones was reluctantly persuaded by Leighton to become an ARA for a few years.

All this expansion of the art world was made possible by one very important person — the Victorian patron. It was the new middle classes, merchants, bankers and industrialists, who were the buyers of Victorian art, and who provided the economic foundations on which the Victorian art world was built. From the start, they distrusted Old Masters as an aristocratic preserve and too prone to fakes and false attributions. They preferred to buy modern works, preferably by British artists, although there were many advanced Victorian collectors of European art as well. Although dealers were important in Victorian times, patrons preferred to deal with the artist direct. The Royal Academy often provided the initial introduction, after which artist and patron often became close friends. Victorian patronage is still a woefully understudied subject, and much research needs to be done. Probably the best-known patrons are those who supported the Pre-Raphaelites — James Leathart, F.R. Leyland, Thomas Plint, and B.G. Windus. It says much for the strength of Victorian patronage that even supposedly advanced or difficult artists nearly always found patrons to support them. Charles Rickards, G.F. Watts's patron, amassed a huge collection of his work, all bought direct from the artist. The majority of Victorian patrons were northerners, from the great industrial towns of the north — Birmingham, Manchester, Liverpool, Bradford, Newcastle. In the nineteenth century, the north was rich and the south was poor.

Another patron was Prince Albert, who was to have an important influence on Victorian patronage and collecting. Both Victoria and Albert were avid collectors of contemporary art and Albert, through his membership of the Fine Arts Commission and other committees, did valuable service in disseminating interest in the arts, in design, and in art education. Government Schools of Art and Design were set up in all the major towns. Public patronage never played an important role, with the exception of the decorations of the Houses of Parliament.

The nineteenth century was the age of the museum. Almost all our major museums, both in London and the provinces, were founded in the Victorian period. The philosophy behind them may have been liberal democracy, but the money to build them was mostly private. Civic pride was a far greater force in the nineteenth century than it is today, and almost all the great provincial museums of England bear the name of a local benefactor.

The Victorians invented the art exhibition as we know it today. The Manchester Art Treasures Exhibition of 1857 was the ancestor of the blockbuster exhibitions of the twentieth century and attracted huge crowds.

The Victorians also invented the art magazine. The *Art-Journal* and *The Studio* were the most successful, but many others, such as *The Athenaeum*, carried lengthy art reviews. The growth of magazines also led to a huge demand for illustrators, and many artists became specialists in this area. It was also a common way for a young artist to become established. Luke Fildes, for example, made his name as the illustrator for Dickens's last, unfinished, novel *Edwin Drood*. The 1860s are recorded as the golden age of the illustrator, but illustration, particularly of children's books, continued to attract many artists throughout the century. In the hands of painters like Arthur Rackham and Edmund Dulac, childrens' books attained levels of beauty, elaboration and quality never equalled since.

Another important Victorian invention was the reproductive engraving. By means of a steel plate, enormous numbers of prints could be made of a picture, and by this means, a whole secondary market was opened up to artists. Frith and Holman Hunt were two artists to benefit enormously from this market; prints of 'The Railway Station' and 'The Light of the World' were Victorian best-sellers. At its height, in the 1850s and 1860s, an artist could sell the reproduction rights for more than the painting itself. Almost all the leading art dealers of the day were also print publishers — Agnew, Graves, Flatou, the Fine Art Society. Prints of famous Victorian pictures found their way into homes, not only in England, but all over the Empire as well. Working Mens' Clubs got up subscriptions to buy them. In this way, art was disseminated to a larger audience than ever before in history. Victorian art was, in truth, popular art, and pictures were more widely discussed, or caricatured in *Punch*, than they are even today, when film, television and other means of communication offer so many rival attractions.

All art is a reflection of its time, and this is especially true of the Victorian period. Victorian art is a mirror in which we can see the tastes, aspirations and prejudices of the Victorians clearly reflected, particularly those of the middle-classes. The extraordinary richness, variety and complexity of Victorian art reflect an equally rich and complex society. Above all it was a literary society. The average businessman in his suburban villa was likely to be well-read, and much of Victorian art is literary in inspiration. Never in art history have art and literature gone so hand-in-hand. The iconography of art was vastly expanded in the nineteenth century, compared to the eighteenth century, when portraits, landscape and historical scenes were the only possible subjects. A whole range of new subject matter was

Colour Plate 2. **JOHN ATKINSON GRIMSHAW.** October Gold

introduced by Victorian painters, particularly in the field of 'modern life' painting. The ambiguous position of women in Victorian society, and their gradual achievement of independent rights, is also reflected in much of their art. These are a few of the reasons why Victorian art is such an absorbing and exciting period to study, and why I have spent twenty-five years or so writing about it.

Victorian Painting 1837-1901

All historical divisions are arbitrary. Nothing in English painting began in 1837 or finished in 1901. Because Queen Victoria gave her name to the age, and ruled for longer than any other English monarch, the main problem of the Victorian period is its length. Sixty-three years, a period covering at least three generations, is far too big a span to embrace any single, easily definable, artistic movement. Even early, mid- and late Victorian will hardly fit as definitions, because the history of Victorian art is so full of complex and overlapping schools, movements and personalities. English art, in any case, has tended to produce individualists who are difficult to fit into any category, particularly in the nineteenth century. Even the term 'Victorian' is itself totally misleading. To describe a picture painted in 1840 and another one painted in 1900 as 'Victorian' is historically meaningless. The word Victorian means as much, or as little, to the nineteenth century as the word Georgian means to the eighteenth. In my own view the Victorians were the heirs of the Romantic movement, and the only satisfactory definition of Victorian art is to see it as a continuing phase of nineteenth century romanticism.

The 1840s

This decade can be described as a watershed; the decade when the Romantic movement came to an end, and the Victorian period began. The artistic scene was still dominated by the mighty Turner, whose late works such as 'Rain, Steam & Speed' of 1844, met with a generally hostile and uncomprehending response. The year before, a young Oxford graduate, John Ruskin (Plate 1), published the first volume of *Modern Painters*, containing his celebrated defence of Turner's late work. Turner died in 1851, the year of the Great Exhibition, a symbol of the new Victorian age. John Martin produced some of his greatest works in the 1840s, in particular the three 'Judgement' pictures, but by this time the vogue for his biblical visions was past, and he died forgotten in 1854. The new Houses of Parliament were completed in the 1840s, and this led to the Westminster Competitions for suitable historical pictures to decorate the new buildings. This was a scheme much encouraged by the young Prince Albert. The prizes were mostly awarded to forgotten nonentities, and the competitions are now chiefly remembered for causing the suicide of the painter Benjamin Robert Haydon, who failed to secure a prize. In general the competitions failed in their aim of encouraging a school of grand historical painting in England. Daniel Maclise and William Dyce painted historical subjects, and made worthwhile contributions to the decorations of the Houses of Parliament, and William Etty continued to paint nudes and mythological subjects until his death in 1849. In the winter of 1848-9 a group of young Royal Academy students founded what was to be the most influential of all Victorian art movements — the Pre-Raphaelite Brotherhood.

Plate 1
GEORGE RICHMOND.
John Ruskin

14

Plate 2. **WILLIAM POWELL FRITH**. Claude Duval

A Novel in a Rectangle — the Vogue for Literary Genre

A growing feature of the 1830s and 1840s was the vogue for literary and historical subjects, especially from the eighteenth century. Painters such as E.M. Ward, C.R. Leslie, and the young Frith were among the countless artists to turn to this new and increasingly popular range of subjects. Their endless scenes from Goldsmith, Boswell, Sterne, or *Le Bourgeois Gentilhomme*, anecdotal, sentimental, humorous, and often exhibited with lengthy quotations, found a ready audience in the newly-rich, novel-reading Victorian middle classes. Thackeray was so irritated by this vogue that he suggested a separate room be set aside at the Royal Academy exhibitions for pictures of the Vicar of Wakefield. It was these pictures that first taught the Victorian public to equate painting with literature, taught them that a picture was something to be read, a novel in a rectangle. This new and specifically Victorian type of narrative picture was a genre that was to remain popular for the rest of the century.

William Powell Frith began his extraordinarily long career exhibiting at the Royal Academy in 1840. During the 1840s he followed the fashion for literary subjects, but also painted scenes of English life in the Tudor and Elizabethan periods. His 'Village Merrymaking' and 'Coming of Age' perfectly encapsulated that Victorian passion for the 'golden, olden tyme' that permeated so much of the art, architecture and literature in the 1830s and 1840s (Plate 2). It was a vogue fuelled by the novels of Walter Scott, and manifested itself in such episodes as the Eglinton Tournament, and the Young England movement. Although Frith was to become famous as a painter of modern life subjects, he continued to paint literary and historical subjects to the end of his career.

Colour Plate 3. **RICHARD DADD.** Contradiction — Oberon and Titania

Fairy Paintings

A curious offshoot of the vogue for literary subjects in the 1840s was the popularity of fairy and fantasy subjects. The most popular sources were Shakespearian — either scenes from *A Midsummer Night's Dream* or *The Tempest*. Edwin Landseer, Daniel Maclise and Robert Huskisson were among the many artists to choose scenes from these plays. So too did the young Richard Dadd, who later went mad and murdered his father. Although confined to mental asylums for the rest of his life, Dadd continued to paint fairy subjects such as 'The Fairy Feller's Master-stroke' and 'Contradiction — Oberon and Titania' (Colour Plate 3). These are among the strangest, and most obsessive of all Victorian paintings. Another artist who made the world of goblins and fantastical creatures his own was John Anster Fitzgerald, the Victorian equivalent of Hieronymus Bosch. The Victorian mania for fairies never died out, particularly in the world of illustrated books for children. It reached its climax in the superb illustrations of Arthur Rackham and Edmund Dulac at the end of the century.

Richard Redgrave and Social Realism

Redgrave began his career as a painter of literary subjects, but his real importance lies in his pioneering of modern life subjects in the 1840s. He was a sensitive man,

Colour Plate 4. **RICHARD REDGRAVE.** The Emigrants' Last Sight of Home

and was appalled by the social evils of the Industrial Revolution, which worried him even as a child. In particular, he was drawn to the lot of oppressed female workers, and this inspired him to paint such pictures as 'The Seamstress', 'Going to Service', and most famous of all 'The Poor Teacher', better known as 'The Governess'. In these pictures he deliberately used modern dress, and avoided the conventions of dressing his figures in historical costume. Redgrave's 'social realist' pictures had a tremendous impact at the time, echoing a parallel literary movement in the 1840s in the novels of Mrs. Gaskell and Charles Kingsley, and above all in Thomas Hood's poem *Song of the Shirt.* This poem was to inspire pictures of overworked and starving steamstresses for the next fifty years. Later, Redgrave became too involved with teaching and administrative duties to have much time for painting, but he did produce some beautiful landscapes inspired by Pre-Raphaelite techniques, and 'The Emigrants' Last Sight of Home' (Colour Plate 4) is one of the most beautiful Victorian pictures on the controversial theme of emigration. Above all, Redgrave deserves recognition as the father of the Victorian 'modern life' school.

William Powell Frith and Victorian 'Modern Life'

The Pre-Raphaelites are often credited with making modern life subjects acceptable. This is a fallacy, and it is to Redgrave that the credit is really due. Of the Pre-Raphaelites, only Holman Hunt and Ford Madox Brown really made any contribution to the genre. The painter who, above all, made 'modern life' popular in the 1850s and 1860s was Frith. It was he who painted its most memorable masterpieces, the three great panoramas of Victorian life: 'Ramsgate Sands', 'Derby Day', and 'The Railway Station'. In his autobiography Frith claims that he was "always strongly drawn to painting modern life", and was also tired of historical subjects.

Frith's 'Ramsgate Sands', or to use its original title, 'Life At the Seaside', was an instant success at the Royal Academy in 1854. The critics were cool and contemptuous, and one referred to it as 'a vulgar piece of cockney business'. Queen Victoria and Prince Albert disagreed, and bought the picture. Modern life pictures were invariably unpopular with the critics and the art world, but hugely popular with the public. Frith went on to even greater success with 'Derby Day' in 1858. This was the first picture to have a rail put up to protect it from the crowds at the Royal Academy since Wilkie's 'Chelsea Pensioners Reading the Waterloo Dispatch' of 1822. Frith's last big panorama was 'The Railway Station' of 1862, showing a crowd about to board a train at Paddington Station. The popularity of his pictures was widely disseminated by the booming market in reproductive engravings. Frith sold 'The Railway Station' including the sketch, and the engraving rights, to the dealer Flatou for £4,500, a huge sum by the standards of the day. Several Victorian painters obtained even higher figures than this.

Frith continued to paint modern life subjects for the next twenty years, interspersed with historical and literary subjects as well. He used exactly the same academic methods for either type of picture, posing models in the studio, making sketches for groups of figures, and then working on the overall composition (Colour Plate 5). He also used working photographs, as did many Victorian artists, and sent Robert Howlett to the Derby to "photograph for him from the roof of a cab as many queer groups of figures as he could".

Frith also painted two important sets of Hogarthian 'moral progress' pictures, entitled 'The Road to Ruin', and 'The Race for Wealth', the first a moral tale about gambling, the second about the Victorian passion for investing in speculative companies. Frith was also commissioned by the dealer Gambart to paint three London scenes for the enormous sum of £10,000, but he had to abandon this in order to paint 'The Marriage of the Prince of Wales' for Queen Victoria. By the late 1880s the vogue for modern life pictures had begun to decline, so Frith consoled himself by writing his autobiography, and making replicas of his earlier works.

Frith's only imitators of note were John Ritchie and George Elgar Hicks, who painted a number of interesting scenes of Victorian life, such as 'The General Post Office at One Minute to Six' (Colour Plate 6), 'Dividend Day at the Bank of England' and 'Billingsgate Market'. Other interesting London street and park scenes were painted by Arthur Boyd Houghton and John Ritchie. Travel by rail or omnibus also featured in many pictures, such as Abraham Solomon's 'First Class' and 'Second Class', and others by Augustus Egg and William Maw Egley. Contemporary events, particularly the Crimean War and the Indian Mutiny, inspired many pictures, the most outstanding being Henry Nelson O'Neil's 'Eastwood Ho! August 1857' and 'Home Again'. The tradition of scenes of Scottish life begun by David Wilkie was carried on by such artists as Thomas Faed. In the 1870s a group of young artists working as illustrators for *The Graphic* magazine began to paint social problem pictures with a new intensity, but these will be dealt with in the section 'High Life and Low Life'. Many artists better known for other subjects occasionally turned to modern life for inspiration, but the vogue for such pictures had begun to decline by the 1880s. Taken as a whole, Victorian modern life painting presents us with a unique, visual social history of the mid-Victorian age. No other period of English art was quite so self-obsessed, or so conscious of its own modernity.

The Pre-Raphaelite Brotherhood

The year 1848 was a year of revolutions and unrest all over Europe. In the autumn and winter of that year, three young Royal Academy students started a revolution in English art that was to reverberate through the rest of the century. Their names were Dante Gabriel Rossetti, William Holman Hunt and John Everett Millais, founders of the Pre-Raphaelite Brotherhood. The origins of the Brotherhood lay in a series of meetings at each other's studios to talk and exchange ideas. Finding that their views coincided, they decided to form themselves into an artistic group. Rossetti added to the conspiratorial excitement by proposing that it be a secret society, known only to its members. The name Pre-Raphaelite was chosen to express the group's admiration for the early Italian painters of the period before Raphael, although none of them had ever been to Italy. Brotherhood was chosen because it made them into a secret, close-knit band of brothers. This was almost certainly inspired by the Nazarenes, a group of intensely serious German artists living in Rome since 1810. It was also decided that they would sign all their pictures with the mysterious initials PRB.

So what were the ideas and aims of the Brotherhood? It has to be realised from the outset that the Pre-Raphaelites were a group of earnest, rebellious, high-spirited, and above all very young men. They were all aged between nineteen and twenty-one, and inevitably their ideas were neither entirely new, nor entirely clear. What united them was their youth, energy and determination to break away from the artistic establishment of the day, and make a fresh start. They were determined, above all, to paint more serious and inspiring subjects than those which were generally found on the walls of the Royal Academy; to study all details from nature; and to develop what they saw as a more honest technique. This led to the practice of painting in pure colours over a wet white ground, which is what gives the pictures of Millais and Holman Hunt, in particular, their startlingly bright appearance.

The question then arose of who else should be invited to join. Ford Madox Brown, the one artist who should have belonged, was opposed by Hunt on grounds of age. Eventually four other friends were invited of whom only one, James Collinson, was a painter. Of the others, Frederick George Stephens and William Michael Rossetti later became critics and writers, and Thomas Woolner was a sculptor.

The Brotherhood effectively came to an end in 1853, so only lasted for a brief four years or so. Just how this motley and haphazard band of youthful rebels completely changed the course of English art is one of the wonders of art history. Never can such an important artistic movement have had such an unpromising beginning.

At first everything went well. In the summer of 1849 the first Pre-Raphaelite pictures were exhibited in public. Rossetti sent his 'The Girlhood of Mary The Virgin' to the Free Exhibition; later Millais and Hunt sent their pictures of 'Isabella' and 'Rienzi' to the Royal Academy. All three pictures were favourably received,

Colour Plate 5. **WILLIAM POWELL FRITH.** Many Happy Returns of the Day

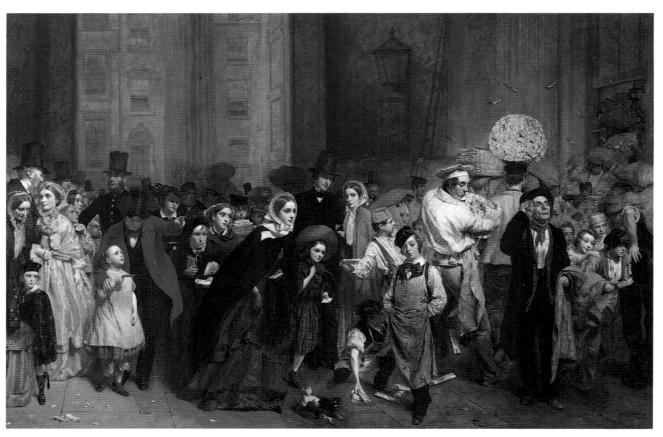

Colour Plate 6. **GEORGE ELGAR HICKS.** The General Post Office at One Minute to Six

Colour Plate 7. **WILLIAM HOLMAN HUNT.** The Hireling Shepherd

and Millais, Hunt and Collinson's pictures at the Academy were all sold. Millais wrote to Rossetti that "the success of the PRB is now quite certain".

This confidence was to be rudely shattered the following year, the main reason being that the secret of the initials PRB leaked out in the art world, mainly due to the publication of *The Germ*, the short-lived magazine of the Brotherhood, of which four issues were published in 1850. It was a literary and artistic magazine, intended as a mouthpiece for the Brotherhood's ideas. Rossetti was the guiding hand behind it and several of his early poems were published in it, along with other contributions from Christina Rossetti, Coventry Patmore and William Bell Scott. Although short lived, *The Germ* did have the effect of publicising the Brotherhood within the art world, with disastrous results. The art establishment, both senior artists and critics, reacted angrily to what they saw as a presumptuous and provocative secret society, aimed deliberately at undermining the establishment's authority, and courting publicity for itself.

As soon as the Pre-Raphaelites began to exhibit their pictures in 1850, the critics turned on them with venom. Rossetti's 'Ecce Ancilla Domini' and W.H. Deverell's 'Twelfth Night' were both attacked at the Free Exhibition, and worse was to come at the Royal Academy. Millais's 'Christ in the House of his Parents' — now known as 'The Carpenter's Shop' — was singled out by *The Times* as "revolting" and the Holy Family as "finished with . . . loathsome minuteness . . . disgusting." Charles Dickens went even further, and in an extraordinary diatribe in *Household Words* wrote that the figure of the mother of Jesus was "a women so hideous in her ugliness that . . . she would stand out from the rest of the company as a Monster, in the vilest cabaret in France, or the lowest gin-shop in England." Later Dickens recanted, and he and Millais became great friends. Other pictures, by Holman Hunt, James Collinson and Charles Alston Collins, fared little better, and none of their pictures were sold.

Recriminations began to break out. Rossetti vowed never to exhibit in public again; Millais's parents accused Rossetti of bringing their brilliant son into disrepute; Hunt was plunged into financial troubles; and James Collinson resigned from the Brotherhood. But the other Pre-Raphaelites determined to stick to their guns, and paint on. At the Royal Academy exhibition of the following year, 1851, they were back in force, with Millais represented by three works 'Mariana' (Colour Plate 13), 'The Woodman's Daughter' and 'The Return of the Dove to the Ark'. Hunt, Madox Brown and C.A. Collins were also represented. Once again, the critics attacked, led by *The Times* whose review was particularly jeering and sarcastic.

But help was at hand, in the shape of John Ruskin, the leading art critic in the land, although then only thirty-two years of age. At the suggestion of the poet Coventry Patmore, he intervened at this crucial moment for the Pre-Raphaelites by writing two letters to *The Times*, praising their pictures and expressing the hope that they "may . . . lay in our England the foundation of a school of art nobler than the world has seen for three hundred years". So great was Ruskin's influence that these two letters, later published in a pamphlet and delivered as lectures, decisively turned the tide in the Pre-Raphaelites' favour. The critics began to be more polite, and younger artists came forward to join the movement. In the following year, 1852, Millais and Hunt showed two of their greatest masterpieces at the RA: 'Ophelia' and 'The Hireling Shepherd' (Colour Plate 7); Ford Madox Brown sent 'Pretty Baa-Lambs' and 'Christ Washing Peter's Feet'. This time the pictures were well received. In Liverpool, Hunt's picture of 'Valentine Rescuing Sylvia' was awarded first prize at the annual exhibition, the first time a Pre-Raphaelite picture had won any kind of award. Liverpool and Manchester were later to prove an important source of patrons, as well as a whole school of disciples and followers.

Ironically, this worldly success coincided with the gradual break-up of the Brotherhood. As we have seen, Collinson had already resigned (after breaking off his engagement to Rossetti's sister Christina). W.H. Deverell and Arthur Hughes were suggested as new members, but the matter lapsed, out of sheer apathy. Meetings became less frequent, and in 1851 William Michael Rossetti gave up his journal of the Brotherhood's proceedings. In 1852 Woolner left for Australia, the event that was to inspire Madox Brown's picture 'The Last of England'. Rossetti was beginning to go his own way, turning to small, intense and romantic watercolours on literary and medieval themes that were to be his greatest contribution to the future of the Pre-Raphaelite movement. In 1851 he began his tragic and obsessive affair with the model Elizabeth Siddal, already the heroine of many Pre-Raphaelite pictures. The affair was to end in their marriage and her suicide, with momentous consequences for the rest of Rossetti's career. In the summer of 1853, Ruskin invited Millais to join him and his wife on a trip to Scotland. This ill-fated holiday, at Glenfinlas, in Perthshire, was to result in Millais's famous portrait of Ruskin standing by a stream, but also led to the break-up of Ruskin's marriage, a scandalous divorce, and Effie Ruskin's eventual marriage to Millais. Later in 1853, Millais was

Plate 3. **DANTE GABRIEL CHARLES ROSSETTI.** Study of Jane Morris

elected an Associate of the Royal Academy, and was thus welcomed to the heart of the establishment, and in 1854, Holman Hunt announced his plans to visit the Middle East in search of inspiration for religious subjects. And so, as Rossetti wrote, "now the whole Round Table is dissolved". The Pre-Raphaelite Brotherhood was at an end. But Pre-Raphaelitism was only just beginning.

Pre-Raphaelite Associates — Ford Madox Brown and Arthur Hughes

During the 1850s and 1860s, a great many younger artists were influenced by the ideas and the inspiration of the Pre-Raphaelite Brotherhood. Of these, the two most important were Ford Madox Brown and Arthur Hughes. Madox Brown never joined the Brotherhood, but was closely involved with them, and could well have been a member. In any case, he was an independent, rather grumpy character, who preferred to work on his own. Brown had trained on the Continent, and was influenced by the Nazarenes in Rome. His first Royal Academy exhibits were ambitious-historical works — 'Wycliffe Reading his Translation of the Bible' and 'Chaucer at the Court of King Edward III'. These pictures have many of the characteristics of the early Brotherhood style — detail, carefully studied costumes, the blend of historicism and nationalism, the idealising of the Middle Ages.

Brown's greatest contribution to Pre-Raphaelitism was in two other areas — social realism and landscape painting. During the 1850s Brown painted his two best-known pictures, 'The Last of England' and 'Work', keyworks in the history of Victorian painting. 'The Last of England' was inspired by Thomas Woolner's departure for Australia in 1852, and Brown worked on it until 1855. The models were himself and his wife Emma, who had to sit for the picture out of doors in all weathers, even with snow on the ground. The red ribbons on her hat took him four weeks to paint. Later Brown wrote of the picture: "Absolutely without regard to the art of any period or country, I have tried to render this scene as it would

Colour Plate 8. **FORD MADOX BROWN.** Work

appear." This statement sums up perfectly the fearlessly honest search for truth so typical of both Brown and the other Pre-Raphaelites, especially Holman Hunt.

Brown was a great admirer of the writer Thomas Carlyle, and what he attempted in his great picture entitled simply 'Work' (Colour Plate 8) is a pictorial representation of Carlyle's social philosophy. All the different classes of Victorian society are represented — manual labourers in the centre, a rich lady and gentleman on horseback, and a middle-class lady distributing temperance tracts, a barefoot flower-seller, sleeping tramps and, leaning on a fence on the right, the intellectuals, Thomas Carlyle, in a hat, and F.D. Maurice, a Christian Socialist and founder of the Working Men's Colleges. It is one of the most intensely didactic, moralistic, and allegorical of all Victorian narrative pictures, and is basically intended to glorify the virtues of work, something which every Victorian believed was the root cause of England's greatness. Although Brown was politically a radical, and there is a strong element of protest in both 'Work' and 'The Last of England', both pictures are more likely to

Colour Plate 9. **ARTHUR HUGHES.** April Love

inspire patriotic feelings than a desire for social revolution.

Next to Madox Brown, Arthur Hughes was the most important Pre-Raphaelite follower outside the Brotherhood. He was converted to Pre-Raphaelitism by reading *The Germ*, and during the 1850s and 1860s he painted a succession of Pre-Raphaelite masterpieces, which can stand comparison with anything produced by the Brotherhood. Hughes was a quiet, self-effacing character, and was content to follow the ideas of others, in particular those of Millais. His forte was romantic figure subjects, set in brilliantly coloured Pre-Raphaelite landscape settings such as 'April Love' (Colour Plate 9), or 'The Long Engagement'. Under Rossetti's influence Hughes also painted some Arthurian subjects, such as 'The Brave Geraint' and 'The Knight of the Sun'. In 1858 Hughes and his family moved out of London, and thereafter he turned increasingly to pictures of children in landscapes, such as 'The Woodman's Child', or 'Home from the Sea'. After the 1860s, his work declines in intensity, but he remained to the end a painter of rare sensibility. He designed for Morris & Co., he produced book illustrations, and painted a number of delightful family portraits, particularly of the family of James Leathart, the great Newcastle collector and patron. Although Hughes broadened his technique in later years, it is to his credit that he remained faithful, like Holman Hunt, to the principles of the Brotherhood.

Some Pre-Raphaelite Followers of the 1850s

As the Pre-Raphaelite movement gathered strength, so the number of its followers and imitators increased. For some, Pre-Raphaelite influence was only a passing phase, resulting in only one or two pictures; but for others, it was more long-lasting. From the start, the Pre-Raphaelite movement split into two main camps: the followers of Millais and Holman Hunt, the hard-edge painters of brightly coloured figures in minutely-detailed landscapes; and the followers of Rossetti, painters of Arthurian and other romantic literary subjects, such as Edward Burne-Jones. It was Rossetti and his followers who were to have much the more long-lasting influence, carrying Pre-Raphaelitism on to the end of the century, and beyond (Plate 3).

During the 1850s, it was the influence of Millais and Holman Hunt which predominated. The main associates of the Brotherhood, as we have already seen, were Ford Madox Brown and Arthur Hughes; other associates were Charles Allston Collins and Walter Howell Deverell. One older artist to fall under the Pre-Raphaelite spell was William Dyce. Like Madox Brown, Dyce was a historical painter, and had studied in Rome with the Nazarenes. Encouraged by Ruskin, he intensified his style, and painted several remarkable Pre-Raphaelite pictures, such as 'Titian's First Essay in Colour' and 'George Herbert at Bemerton'. He also contributed much to the development of Pre-Raphaelite landscape painting, which is dealt with in the next section.

For Henry Wallis, Pre-Raphaelitism was only a brief phase, but it did result in two memorable masterpieces, 'The Death of Chatterton' and 'The Stonebreaker' (Plate 4). In the former, the model for the figure of the dead boy poet was the novelist, George Meredith. Subsequently, Henry Wallis eloped with Meredith's wife, an exact repetition of the Millais-Ruskin scenario. 'The Stonebreaker', exhibited with a quotation from Carlyle, is one of the gloomiest of all Victorian social realist pictures, showing a stonebreaker who has died at his work.

By a strange coincidence, Wallis's 'The Stonebreaker' was exhibited at the Royal Academy in 1858, together with a very much more cheerful version of the same subject by John Brett. Brett's 'The Stonebreaker' shows a boy lazily breaking stones in a landscape of sunny, Pre-Raphaelite brilliance, painted near Box Hill in Surrey. For Brett, Pre-Raphaelitism was to have long-lasting and fruitful results. Ruskin praised Brett's 'The Stonebreaker' at the Academy, and proceeded to take the young artist under his wing. Thereafter, Brett's main contribution to Pre-Raphaelitism was as a landscape painter. As we have seen, Richard Redgrave, the painter of social realist pictures in the 1840s, turned in the 1850s to Pre-Raphaelite landscape.

Many narrative pictures of the 1850s show Pre-Raphaelite influence. A typical example is 'The Last Day in the Old Home' by Robert Braithwaite Martineau, a friend and pupil of Holman Hunt. Like Hunt, Martineau was interested in allegories of modern life with a moral message, such as Hunt's 'The Awakening Conscience'. 'The Last Day in the Old Home' shows a feckless aristocrat, having gambled away the family fortune, drinking a last glass of champagne in the ancestral home. One could cite many other examples, such as Henry Bowler's 'The Doubt — "Can These Dry Bones Live?" ' or 'The Talking Oak' by William Maw Egley.

The Pre-Raphaelites also made important converts in the provinces. In Newcastle, William Bell Scott, master of the local Government School of Design, was an early friend of the Brotherhood, and contributor to *The Germ*. His most famous picture is 'Iron and Coal', showing the industrial and commercial life of Tyneside. Further north in Scotland, the most notable Pre-Raphaelite follower was Sir Joseph Noel Paton. During the 1850s he produced some outstanding pictures, such as 'Hesperus' or 'The Bluidie Tryst'. He also painted fairy pictures, historical subjects, and later, mainly religious works. Liverpool was by far the biggest source of patrons and followers, the most interesting of the latter being William Lindsay Windus, painter of 'Burd Helen' and 'Too Late'. Others included James Campbell, John Lee, William Huggins, and numerous landscape painters.

Colour Plate 10. **WILLIAM DYCE.** Pegwell Bay

The Pre-Raphaelite Landscape

From the start, landscape was a key element in the Pre-Raphaelite style. The determination of the Pre-Raphaelites to paint everything with complete fidelity is reflected most clearly in their approach to landscape. Although Ruskin did not become aware of the Pre-Raphaelites until 1850, they were already familiar with his writings. Holman Hunt, in particular, had read *Modern Painters* in 1847, and felt that it had been "written expressly for him". No doubt he had in mind Ruskin's famous and much-quoted exhortation to the young artists of England to "go to Nature in all singleness of heart, and walk with her laboriously and trustingly . . . rejecting nothing, selecting nothing, and scorning nothing". The biblical tone of this passage is typical of Ruskin's passionate and mystical reverence for nature. An artist simply had to put his trust in nature, and nature would take him by the hand and show him the way. For Ruskin, nature was a kind of holy book wherein the good student might read, learn, and seek guidance. This incredibly earnest, didactic approach to art was shared by the Pre-Raphaelite Brotherhood. A picture did not have to be merely pretty, but to do good. A Ruskinian landscape was a moral

Colour Plate 11. **JOHN BRETT.** Val d'Aosta

landscape. Ruskin was to become the chief advocate of Pre-Raphaelite landscape painting, supporting and encouraging it in his annual *Academy Notes*.

Neither Hunt nor Millais were ever pure landscape painters, but landscape backgrounds were a key element in all their Pre-Raphaelite pictures. In order to achieve total fidelity, they believed in taking their canvases out of doors, and painting on the spot, in full sunlight. Combined with their technique of painting in pure colours over a wet, white ground, this was an incredibly slow and laborious method of painting. A whole day's work might result in only a few square inches of paint. This relentless, microscopic approach to landscape resulted in an over-accumulation of detail at the expense of the overall composition, a common fault with Pre-Raphaelite landscapes. The lack of shadows also tended to produce an airless, artificial atmosphere that to twentieth century eyes looks more surrealistic than realistic. But while it lasted the Pre-Raphaelite experiment breathed new vitality and intensity into Victorian landscape painting, and produced such masterpieces as Millais's 'Ophelia'* and Hunt's 'The Hireling Shepherd' (Colour Plate 7). Even after Pre-Raphaelite influences declined in the 1860s and 1870s, many landscape painters, especially watercolourists such as Birket Foster, continued to imitate their style and methods. After the Pre-Raphaelites, English landscape painting was never the same again.

Ford Madox Brown was the only major Pre-Raphaelite to devote himself to pure landscape. The best of his landscapes was 'An English Autumn Afternoon', which he painted from the back window of his house in Hampstead. In the 1850s he painted a number of small landscape studies in the countryside around London. These are painted with the uncompromising honesty and lack of sentimentality so typical of the man and his work, and they had a great influence on other Pre-Raphaelite landscape painters, especially John Brett and Thomas Seddon, and the Liverpool painters such as Daniel Alexander Williamson and William Davis.

A number of older artists were converted to Pre-Raphaelite landscape, notably William Dyce, painter of the extraordinary 'Pegwell Bay' (Colour Plate 10). William Bell Scott also painted some fine landscapes, especially sunsets (Plate 5), and a more surprising convert was the topographer and nonsense poet Edward Lear, who was so impressed with Hunt's 'The Hireling Shepherd' that he asked Hunt, fifteen years his junior, to give him painting lessons. Another disciple of Hunt was Thomas Seddon who accompanied him on his first trip to the Holy Land and painted a small number of middle eastern landscapes before his early death in 1856.

John Brett and John William Inchbold can conveniently be grouped together, as they were both young artists who felt the full force of Ruskin's encouragement. Inchbold was born in Leeds in 1830, and was converted to the Pre-Raphaelite style in the 1850s. His earliest works, such as 'Early Spring', are of outstanding quality, and were regularly praised by Ruskin in *Academy Notes*. Inchbold, like Ruskin, was an admirer of Wordsworth, and frequently gave his pictures Wordsworthian titles. Ruskin encouraged Inchbold to visit Switzerland, but was then disappointed with the pictures he painted there. Exactly the same thing happened with John Brett. After praising Brett's 'The Stonebreaker', Ruskin suggested that he go and paint the Val d'Aosta (Colour Plate 11). Brett dutifully obliged, and when Ruskin saw the finished result, he complained that it was lacking in grandeur. Perhaps Ruskin had

Plate 5. **WILLIAM BELL SCOTT.** The Gloaming — a Manse Garden in Berwickshire

at last realised that romantic grandeur and factual detail were incompatible, and that a totally Ruskinian landscape was an impossibility, for in 1859 he gave up his *Academy Notes*. Both Inchbold and Brett continued painting, and Brett produced several more outstanding Pre-Raphaelite works. Later he turned mostly to coastal scenes. Inchbold's fellow-Leeds artist, Atkinson Grimshaw, also painted a number of remarkable landscapes under Pre-Raphaelite influence in the 1860s.

Many other friends and associates of the Pre-Raphaelites painted landscape, some of them only occasionally. Among them was George Price Boyce, friend and neighbour of Rossetti in Chelsea, and Thomas Matthews Rooke, who was commissioned by Ruskin to paint old buildings on the Continent. Waller Hugh Paton, the brother of Sir Joseph Noel Paton, devoted most of his career to landscape, in both oil and watercolour. Many other artists are remembered only for a brief mention in *Academy Notes*, such as J.M. Carrick, J.S. Raven, and E.G. Warren. By far the biggest concentration of Pre-Raphaelite landscape painters was to be found in Liverpool. Among the best were William Davis, J.E. Newton and D.A. Williamson. There were also a number of fine watercolourists, in particular Alfred William Hunt.

By the 1870s the Pre-Raphaelite style of landscape painting began to fall out of favour, partly because of Ruskin's disillusionment, but also because it was so laborious and slow. Also, new influences were at work, mainly from France, all moving more in the direction of naturalism and impressionism. In terms of the English landscape tradition, as exemplified by Constable, Turner and David Cox, Pre-Raphaelite landscape was something of an aberration. By breaking with tradition, and insisting on total realism, it had condemned itself to a dead end. But while it lasted, it produced some of the most extraordinary landscapes in English art, and among watercolour painters its influence survived for much longer.

Colour Plate 12. **DANTE GABRIEL CHARLES ROSSETTI.** Beata Beatrix

The Tragic Pre-Raphaelite — Dante Gabriel Rossetti 1828-1882

Rossetti finally married his mistress and model, Elizabeth Siddal, in 1860. But the marriage was never a happy one, and in 1862 poor Lizzie committed suicide by taking an overdose of laudanum. After this tragedy, Rossetti was a haunted man. He moved away from his old studio, and bought Tudor House in Cheyne Walk, Chelsea. Still tormented by remorse and insomnia, he became increasingly eccentric and reclusive. The bohemian disorder of Tudor House has itself become part of the Pre-Raphaelite legend. Various people lived there, various models came and went, and the sinister Charles Howell became Rossetti's unofficial agent and dealer. It was he who persuaded Rossetti to have Lizzie Siddal's grave dug up and the manuscript poems, which the distraught Rossetti had buried with her, removed from her coffin. These poems, including *The Blessed Damozel,* were later published. In spite of all this, Rossetti remained a fascinating, witty and intelligent man, and cast his spell over many younger artists. Tudor House became a focus for many of the artistic movements of the 1860s and 1870s.

Rossetti's creative genius was far from exhausted. He continued to write and paint for the last twenty years of his life. He began to paint increasingly in oils, and on a larger scale, abandoning the small watercolours of the 1850s. His most famous picture of the 1860s is the haunting 'Beata Beatrix' (Colour Plate 12), a portrait of his dead wife. From then on there was to be one subject, and one subject alone, in Rossetti's art — women. Rossetti was a love painter and a love poet, and there was no greater worshipper of female beauty in English art.

Rossetti's later pictures are almost all half-length figures of girls, or groups of girls, and are quite unique in English art. Painted in rich, voluptuous colour, which reflects the growing influence of the Italian Renaissance, they exude an atmosphere of dreamy, exotic sensuality. The muse of Rossetti's later years was Jane Morris (Plate 3), wife of William Morris, and she was the model for many of these later works, such as 'Prosperina', or 'Astarte Syriaca'. Another of his favourite models was Alexa Wilding who posed for 'The Blessed Damozel', one of the greatest of his later works. By the late 1870s, Rossetti's health was in serious decline, and his consumption of drugs had reached appalling levels. At last, in 1882, he died, paralysed and partially deaf, at the age of only fifty-four. It was a tragic end for the one truly original genius of the Pre-Raphaelite movement.

The Faithful Pre-Raphaelite — William Holman Hunt 1827-1910

Meanwhile, Holman Hunt, Rossetti's old friend and colleague, was pursuing his own very individual path. He was to live to a ripe old age, and became much more famous and successful in his lifetime than Rossetti. This was mainly due to his reputation as a serious religious painter, and the countless prints and engravings made after his work. Of all the original Pre-Raphaelites, it was Holman Hunt who remained most faithful to the Brotherhood's original principles. All his later pictures are developments of ideas formulated much earlier. Although Hunt lacked the imagination of Rossetti and the technical brilliance of Millais, he made up for it in determination, tenacity, and almost superhuman patience. Some of his major religious pictures took five or ten years to complete.

In 1853 Hunt painted his last pictures before the Brotherhood dissolved, 'The

Awakening Conscience' and 'The Light of the World', intended as secular and religious versions on the theme of faith. In both pictures, Hunt used objects to build up a pattern of elaborate symbolic detail. 'The Awakening Conscience', showing a kept woman and her lover in their love-nest, was almost the only Victorian picture to attempt to grapple with the unmentionable problem of prostitution. 'The Light of the World' was to become one of the best-known of all English religious images, an icon of Victorian faith. Both pictures represent the moralising, Ruskinian side of the Pre-Raphaelites, of which Hunt was always the chief exponent. For Hunt, and other serious mid-Victorian artists like him, a picture had no business being pretty or sentimental, it had to do good, to inspire, preach, and uplift. Hunt's pictures are sermons in paint.

In 1854, Hunt set off on the first of several trips to the Holy Land, in search of authentic settings and details for more biblical subjects. The first of these was the extraordinary 'The Scapegoat' of 1854, painted on the shores of the Dead Sea. Hunt became fascinated by Jewish customs and history, as is reflected in his later works, such as 'The Finding of the Saviour in the Temple', 'The Triumph of the Innocents', and 'The Shadow of the Cross'. These great pictures, so redolent of Victorian religiosity, are still difficult for sceptical twentieth century viewers to understand or sympathise with. Hunt's reputation can rest secure, however, on his last great work, 'The Lady of Shalott'. He began the picture in 1856, and was still working on it when be began to go blind in 1905. In this wonderful picture his own brand of elaborate symbolism, decorative richness and the swirling Art Nouveau figure of the red-haired model, are all successfully combined to produce a uniquely powerful and effective image. In his own highly individual way, Hunt was one of the great originals of English nineteenth century art.

The Fickle Pre-Raphaelite — John Everett Millais 1829-1896
1853 was a dramatic year for Millais. Not only did he make the ill-fated trip to Scotland with the Ruskins, but in that year he was elected an Associate of the Royal Academy. This was the first step on the road to joining the artistic establishment. He was to become a full RA in 1863, and eventually its President in 1896, only a few months before his death. He was also the first English artist to be made a baronet, in 1885.

Millais did not immediately abandon Pre-Raphaelite principles after 1853. The process was a gradual one, and during the 1850s he painted some of his most beautiful pictures (Colour Plate 13). 'The Order of Release', which contains a portrait of Effie Ruskin, was painted in 1853. In 1854 he finished the portrait of Ruskin begun at Glenfinlas in Scotland. Despite the affair between Millais and Effie, Ruskin insisted on the portrait being completed. In the following year, after a scandalous divorce case, Millais and Effie Ruskin were married. The Royal Academy exhibition of 1856 was a vintage year for Millais, who exhibited three outstanding pictures — 'The Blind Girl', 'Autumn Leaves' and 'Peace Concluded'. The first two are among the most beautiful of all Millais's pictures, and Ruskin compared 'Autumn Leaves' to the work of the Venetian painter Giorgione. There is certainly enough poetry, mystery, and beautiful colour about it to make the comparison apt. In 1857 came 'Sir Isumbras at the Ford', and in 1859, 'The Vale of

Colour Plate 13. **JOHN EVERETT MILLAIS.** Mariana

Rest', perhaps Millais's last truly Pre-Raphaelite picture. With 'The Black Brunswicker' of 1860, Millais had begun to move towards more obviously popular subjects, and towards a broader technique.

His marriage almost certainly contributed to this change. The couple soon began to raise a large family, and Millais needed to produce more pictures, faster. The Pre-Raphaelite technique was too time-consuming, and Millais wrote that he could no longer afford to spend all day painting an area "no larger than a five-shilling piece". Eventually he changed to a broader, looser style more reminiscent of Reynolds and Gainsborough, both artists he was later to admire and emulate.

Millais's later career belongs to the mainstream of Victorian art rather than to Pre-Raphaelitism. As a painter of portraits, historical pictures, and sentimental pictures of children, he was to be financially more successful and more popular than any of his fellow Pre-Raphaelites. At the height of his fame, he could earn over £30,000 a year, a colossal sum in those days. Until recently, it has been fashionable to dismiss his later work, especially such chestnuts as his 'Bubbles'. But this viewpoint is no longer tenable. Some of his portraits, such as 'Hearts are Trumps', 'Louise Jopling' or 'Mr. Gladstone', are among the finest portraits in Victorian art. Both as a Pre-Raphaelite, and in his later years, Millais was one of the most brilliant artists of the Victorian age.

Pre-Raphaelitism and the Aesthetic Movement

By 1860 the first phase of the Pre-Raphaelite movement was over. The second phase of the movement really begins with the association of three artists — Rossetti, William Morris and Edward Burne-Jones. Under their combined influence, the movement was given a new impetus and direction, carrying it far beyond painting, into almost every aspect of Victorian artistic life — furniture, the decorative arts, architecture and interior decoration, book design and illustration, even literature. For the rest of the century, Pre-Raphaelitism was to become part of the English way of life. After fifty years of neglect in the first half of the twentieth century, it has become an integral part of English culture once again.

The 1860s was a period of intense artistic and intellectual ferment, and out of it emerged the Aesthetic Movement, which was to shape the course of English art for the rest of the century. It also strongly influenced the way in which Pre-Raphaelitism developed, because the Aesthetic Movement was, by its very nature, highly eclectic, and drew on a wide variety of sources of inspiration. Pre-Raphaelitism from 1860 onwards has to be seen as one element in the Aesthetic Movement, and therefore this second phase of the movement is much more complex than the first. At first the dominating figure was Rossetti, but as his health declined the leadership passed to Burne-Jones, whose greatest triumph was the opening of the Grosvenor Gallery in 1877, where he was hailed as England's leading modern artist. Burne-Jones's style was a highly personal but typically aesthetic mixture of Pre-Raphaelite, Italianate and classical elements. He remained faithful to the romantic, Rossettian brand of Pre-Raphaelitism, and at the end of his life was still painting stories from his beloved *Morte d'Arthur*. The influence of Burne-Jones on other English artists was immense, and continued well into the twentieth century.

Parallel with Burne-Jones and the later Pre-Raphaelites, another movement emerged from the 1860s, in direct opposition to Pre-Raphaelitism. This was the Classical Movement, whose leader was Frederic Leighton. His aim was to lead English art back to its European, classical heritage, and after he became President of the Royal Academy in 1878, the English art world divided into two camps, the Academy championing the classical and more traditional artists, and the Grosvenor representing Burne-Jones, Whistler, and the more progressive elements of the Aesthetic Movement. But the Classical Movement was only another facet of the Aesthetic Movement. Burne-Jones and Leighton were both high Victorian aesthetes, one dreaming of Avalon, the other of Parnassus. In the work of many later Victorian artists, Pre-Raphaelite, classical and aesthetic elements are fused in various degrees, which is what makes it such a complex and fascinating period. In the much-quoted words of Henry James, writing about Burne-Jones in 1877: "It is the art of culture, of reflection, of intellectual luxury, of aesthetic refinement . . ." This was the high water-mark of Victorian civilisation, to be swept away by modernism and the First World War.

The Palace of Art — William Morris

Morris and Burne-Jones first met, appropriately in Oxford, most medieval of English towns. It is no coincidence, therefore, that their main contribution to Pre-Raphaelitism was to lead English art and design back to the spirit of the Middle Ages. Morris was to become a designer, Burne-Jones a painter, and their life-long artistic collaboration is a key element in the history of English nineteenth century art.

During their time at Oxford, Morris and Burne-Jones formed part of a circle of high-minded and idealistic young men, united by their enthusiasm for poetry, the Middle Ages and Gothic architecture, and their hatred of the industrial revolution, materialism, trains and just about everything in the nineteenth century. They read Keats, Shelley, Tennyson, Chaucer and, above all, Malory's *Morte d'Arthur,* the book which more than any other was to inspire the work of the later Pre-Raphaelite painters. Among modern writers they read Carlyle and, of course, Ruskin, from whom they learnt of the existence of the Pre-Raphaelite Brotherhood. The artist above all that they wanted to meet was Rossetti.

In 1855 Morris and Burne-Jones left Oxford, by this time having decided to dedicate their lives to the arts. Morris entered the office of the architect G.E. Street, and Burne-Jones became Rossetti's pupil. Later they shared the same rooms in Red Lion Square, Soho, that had been occupied by Rossetti and W.H. Deverell in the historic days of the Pre-Raphaelite Brotherhood. The year 1857 saw the celebrated episode of the Oxford murals, the last and happiest of the Pre-Raphaelite group efforts. The group was commissioned to paint a series of ten murals on the ceiling of the Oxford Union, and chose to paint scenes from the *Morte d'Arthur.* Rossetti was the ringleader, assisted by a group of younger artists, including Burne-Jones, Morris, Arthur Hughes and Val Prinsep. Great fun was had by all, but sadly the murals are today almost totally faded, and very little remains to show of that happy and high-spirited summer of 1857.

The Oxford episode did, however, have other important results. Morris met the beautiful Jane Burden, later to become his wife (Plate 3). After their marriage they decided to build a house of their own, in which everything would be designed and made by them and their friends. This was the now famous Red House at Bexley in Kent, designed by Philip Webb. It was to be their Palace of Art. With his usual prodigious energy and enthusiasm, Morris set about designing everything — furniture, carpets, tapestries, stained glass and metalwork. It was out of all this activity that the celebrated firm of Morris, Marshall & Faulkner & Co. was born. (Later the name was shortened to Morris & Co.) Morris and Burne-Jones were the most important designers, but almost everyone in the Pre-Raphaelite circle became involved — Madox Brown, Arthur Hughes, and William De Morgan, who was in charge of tiles and ceramics. This involvement of artists in design and decorative work was Morris's most vital contribution to the second phase of Pre-Raphaelitism. Almost single-handedly, William Morris, most remarkable of the Victorian polymaths, revolutionised English taste, and founded what is now referred to as the Arts and Crafts Movement. On top of it all, he was a prolific poet, an early socialist, and latterly the founder of the Kelmscott Press. In 1896, the year of his death, he and Burne-Jones produced their finest book, *The Kelmscott Chaucer*, which the poet W.B. Yeats described as "the most beautiful book in the world".

Edward Burne-Jones 1833-1898

Burne-Jones was the most important artist of the second generation of Pre-Raphaelites, and one of the major English artists of the nineteenth century. Born in Birmingham, he began to draw early in life, and was also a voracious reader, especially of romantic poetry. The other great influence in his life was John Henry Newman, so when Burne-Jones went up to Oxford, he intended to enter the church. Although he never became a clergyman, his early vocation left its mark. Like so many Victorians who lost their faith, he transmuted his religious ideals into artistic ones. For him, beauty was his goddess; beauty was synonymous with truth and goodness; it was the Holy Grail. Although Burne-Jones was to become a leader of the Aesthetic Movement, he could never totally accept its philosophy that art existed only for art's sake, and for no other purpose. Burne-Jones was a typically earnest, mid-Victorian moralist who wanted to improve the lot of mankind, and believed that art could achieve this. There was a kind of missionary fervour about him that remained to the end of his life.

By the time he left Oxford in 1855, Burne-Jones had already decided to become a painter. In London, he went to hear his hero, Rossetti, lecture at the Working Men's College. The met, and soon after Rossetti declared that young Ned Jones was "one of the nicest young fellows in Dreamland", and agreed to take him on as a pupil. Under Rossetti's direction, he began to make pen and ink drawings, mostly of medieval subjects, in the spiky, Gothic style of Rossetti's work at this period. In 1858, Burne-Jones lived for a while at Little Holland House, home of the motherly and hospitable Mrs. Prinsep, and here he came under the influence of another member of the household, George Frederick Watts. Watts encouraged Burne-Jones to study the Elgin Marbles, and look at Italian art in order to broaden his outlook and develop his style. He also encouraged him to make his first visit to Italy in 1859. By 1860, he was beginning to work in watercolour, and 'Sidonia von Bork' shows just how fast he was developing his own style.

Burne-Jones was to make three more trips to Italy, with Ruskin in 1862, and again in 1871 and 1873. These trips were to have an immense influence on his development; indeed the Italian influence was to become a key element in his style, as is already evident in 'The Madness of Sir Tristram' of 1862. Like both Watts and Ruskin, Burne-Jones was a great admirer of the Venetian school, especially Titian, Giorgione, Tintoretto and Carpaccio, but he also admired the work of Botticelli, Mantegna, Leonardo and Michelangelo. Like all great artists, he had great powers of assimilation, and during the 1860s he was able to forge all these influences — Italianate, classical, and Pre-Raphaelite — into a unique style of his own.

Another key element in Burne-Jones's style was his involvement in design and decorative work for Morris & Co. From the start, he was the firm's most prolific designer, and as a result there is a constant interaction between his design work and his paintings. Nearly all his pictures have their origin in designs for some other

Colour Plate 14. **EDWARD BURNE-JONES.**
Study for the Sleeping Princess in the Briar Rose series

medium, either stained glass, tapestries, tiles, mosaics, books, furniture, or embroidery. His set of four pictures of 'Pygmalion' for example, started life as illustrations for Morris's poem *The Earthly Paradise*. Although the subject is classical, Burne-Jones has invested his Pygmalion story with an atmosphere of medieval courtly love.

Between 1868 and 1871 Burne-Jones was involved in a romance of his own, with the beautiful Greek sculptress Maria Zambaco. He made many beautiful drawings of her, and she also appears in many of his pictures, such as 'Phyllis and Demophoön'. When this picture was shown at the Old Watercolour Society in 1870, the nude figures were criticised on the grounds of indecency. Burne-Jones indignantly withdrew his picture, and resigned from the Society. In 1871 Robert Buchanan's notorious tirade against Rossetti and his circle, *The Fleshly School of Poetry*, was published and Burne-Jones too must have felt under attack. In 1873 the unfortunate Simeon Solomon, a brilliant young artist friend of both Rossetti and Burne-Jones, was arrested on charges of indecency, and became a complete social outcast. The Palace of Art was under siege. Burne-Jones withdrew from all exhibitions, working entirely for a few loyal patrons.

This was all to change in 1877 with the opening of the Grosvenor Gallery, the brain-child of a rich artistic couple, Sir Coutts Lindsay and his wife Blanche. Situated in a fine Italianate building in Bond Street, the gallery was intended to rival the Royal Academy, and to promote the more progressive artists of the day, both English and European. Burne-Jones was persuaded to send in eight works, which were all hung together on one wall. They included some of his finest works of the 1870s, including 'The Days of Creation', 'The Beguiling of Merlin' and the 'The Mirror of Venus' (Plate 6). Out of the artistic melting-pot of the 1860s Burne-Jones had at last forged his own unique brand of Pre-Raphaelitism. The public and the critics were bowled over. They suddenly realised they had a genius in their midst. Overnight Burne-Jones became famous, and was hailed as one of England's leading artists. Henry James, in his review of the 1877 exhibition, singled out Burne-Jones's paintings as the outstanding pictures in the show, and wrote that "in the palace of art there are many chambers, and that of which Mr. Burne-Jones holds the key is a wondrous museum."

Burne-Jones's picture 'The Mirror of Venus' might serve as a typical example of his mature style. The draperies are classical, the title is Venus, the figures are Botticellian, and the colours Italianate, yet the whole conception is unmistakably aesthetic and Victorian. The mood, as in so much of Burne-Jones's work, is overwhelmingly nostalgic and wistful. 'The Mirror of Venus' could well fit Burne-Jones's own often-quoted definition: "I mean by a picture a beautiful romantic dream of something that never was, never will be — in a light better than any light that ever shone — in a land no-one can define, or remember, only desire . . ." It is a deliberately romantic, introspective art, arousing a mood of nostalgia and reverie. It was a mood common to late Victorian art, and especially the work of the later Pre-Raphaelites.

Success came late to Burne-Jones. In 1877 he was already in his mid-forties. For the next twenty years he was to concentrate on painting ever-larger and more ambitious pictures, and two great cycles of pictures — 'The Perseus' and 'Briar

Rose' series (Colour Plate 14). During the 1880s he continued to develop many of the themes that had already preoccupied him for the past twenty years. He painted classical subjects, such as 'The Garden of Pan' and 'Danae and the Brazen Tower'; he also painted occasional religious subjects, such as 'The Annunciation' of 1879. But as he grew older, he tended to revert increasingly to medieval and Arthurian legends, the great inspiration of his youth. This was to result in some of his finest late works, such as 'King Cophetua and the Beggar Maid' and 'The Last Sleep of Arthur in Avalon'. Parallel with this was a preoccupation with fairy tales, such as the 'Briar Rose' series which is based on the story of the Sleeping Beauty, or subjects based on his own private dream world, such as 'The Golden Stairs'.

Burne-Jones always remained something of an outsider. He was elected an

Plate 6. **EDWARD BURNE-JONES**. The Mirror of Venus

Associate of the Royal Academy in 1885, but only exhibited there once, and resigned in 1893. He remained faithful to the Grosvenor Gallery until its closure in 1887, and then transferred his allegiance to the New Gallery in Regent Street. It was here that he exhibited many of his finest late works, such as 'Love and the Pilgrim' and 'The Wedding of Psyche'. In this last phase his work became increasingly austere, monumental and withdrawn, the colours harder and more metallic, at times almost monochromatic. It was as if Burne-Jones was withdrawing into the recesses of his own dream world. Like so many Victorian moralists, he felt a sense of failure and disappointment. Art had done nothing to check the spread of materialism and ugliness in the nineteenth century. The decadence of the 1890s appalled him, particularly Aubrey Beardsley's illustrations to his beloved *Morte d'Arthur*. Nonetheless, by the end of his career, his work was known and admired all over Europe — even as far afield as Barcelona, where the young Picasso admired his pictures in the pages of the *Studio* magazine. In England, too, he had many imitators and followers, who carried his style and his ideas well into the twentieth century.

Some Pre-Raphaelite Followers 1860-1890

Rossetti died in 1882, William Morris in 1896, Burne-Jones in 1898. All three had tremendous influence on other artists during their lifetimes, and Pre-Raphaelite influence is detectable in English art right up to 1914, and even beyond into the 1920s. Some of these followers were only brief converts to Pre-Raphaelitism; many adapted Pre-Raphaelite ideas and grafted them to their own; some admired Rossetti, others were more attracted to Burne-Jones.

One of Rossetti's most devoted followers was Frederick Sandys. Most of his pictures, like Rossetti's, are half-length figures of beautiful, red-haired, and usually destructive women — 'Medea', 'Fair Rosamund', 'La Belle Ysonde', or 'Queen Eleanor' (Colour Plate 15). Unlike Rossetti, Sandys was a superb technician, and his mastery of Pre-Raphaelite technique was equal to that of Millais or Holman Hunt. He was also a brilliant portrait painter, both in oil or in chalk.

Another artist to fall under Rossetti's spell, but with disastrous consequences, was Simeon Solomon, one of a talented family of Jewish artists. During the 1860s he became part of the Pre-Raphaelite circle, and produced a quantity of brilliantly precocious drawings, gouaches, and oil paintings, mainly of religious subjects involving Judaic ritual. He also painted classical and allegorical subjects, which combine Pre-Raphaelite and aesthetic ideas in a highly individual way. Unfortunately, he also began to explore the forbidden subjects of homosexuality and lesbianism, both of which feature, more or less overtly, in such pictures as 'Sappho and Erinna at Mytelene'. In February 1873 he was arrested for homosexual offences, after which he was shunned by many of his former friends, including

Colour Plate 15. **ANTHONY FREDERICK AUGUSTUS SANDYS.** Queen Eleanor

Swinburne, whose corrupting influence had been a contributory factor to his downfall. Thereafter, Solomon's career drifted on a downward path of drink and destitution, and he ended his days as an alcoholic in the St. Giles Workhouse in 1905. In his later years he continued to produce drawings and pastels, mostly heads of a peculiarly androgynous type, which are not up to the standard of his 1860s work. Solomon's career was one of the minor tragedies of the Pre-Raphaelite movement, and reminds one just how powerful the mid-Victorian moral code was, even in supposedly artistic circles.

Other members of the Rossetti circle were Maria Spartali, who painted Rossettian female figures, and Henry Holiday, painter of the well-known 'Dante and Beatrice', a familiar image due to its endless reproduction in Victorian history books and anthologies. Various provincial artists fell under Pre-Raphaelite influence, such as Frederic J. Shields of Manchester, and Atkinson Grimshaw of Leeds (Colour Plate 2). Shields was both deeply religious and a socialist, and his pictures are mostly either biblical subjects, or strongly social realist scenes of modern life. Grimshaw's earliest pictures, of the early 1860s, are Pre-Raphaelite landscapes, painted under the influence of another Leeds artist John William Inchbold. Later in the 1860s he began to paint the moonlit landscapes for which he is now best known. In the 1870s he also painted a number of romantic figure subjects, such as 'The Lady of Shalott' and 'Elaine', based on Tennyson's poems.

As Rossetti became more and more of a recluse in the 1870s, it was inevitable that the leadership of the Pre-Raphaelites should pass to Burne-Jones. His house in Fulham, The Grange, became increasingly a focal point for young artists during the 1870s and 1880s. The followers of Burne-Jones have tended to be lumped together, and dismissed by most critics as mere imitators. It is now clear, however, that many of them developed distinct artistic personalities of their own.

This is particularly true of two of Burne-Jones's pupils, Thomas Matthews Rooke and John Melhuish Strudwick, both of whom produced their own highly personal versions of the Burne-Jones style. Much the same could be said of John Roddam Spencer-Stanhope and his niece, Evelyn De Morgan. Spencer-Stanhope was a rich dilettante who lived mainly in Florence, and his pictures reflect his obvious admiration for Florentine Renaissance art, especially that of Botticelli. Evelyn De Morgan's pictures are mostly large and complex allegories, painted in a rich and highly-wrought style. Very similar is the work of the Birmingham artist, Sidney Harold Meteyard. Another fervent admirer of Burne-Jones was Walter Crane, later famous as a designer and illustrator of children's books. All these artists produced their own versions of the Burne-Jones idiom, and their work is often linked with that of the European Symbolist painters. There is certainly an affinity there, but Symbolism in English art is a notoriously difficult thing to define. If one accepts that the work of Burne-Jones and G.F. Watts contains elements of symbolism, then it follows that the work of their pupils does too. But a better definition is 'The Last Romantics', the title of an exhibition of late nineteenth century art held at the Barbican Art Gallery in 1989. As the exhibition revealed, the number of artists following Burne-Jones's ideal of romantic, figurative art is endless, and lasted well into the twentieth century, influencing even such unlikely figures as Paul Nash and Stanley Spencer.

John William Waterhouse 1849-1917

The greatest of the late Victorian romantic painters after Burne-Jones was John William Waterhouse. As with so many late nineteenth century painters, Waterhouse painted both Pre-Raphaelite and classical subjects, and is perhaps the only artist to have successfully reconciled these two opposing forces in late Victorian art. Many contemporary critics observed that Waterhouse's style was a very individual fusion of the classicism of Leighton and the aesthetic Pre-Raphaelitism of Burne-Jones.

Waterhouse was a typical late Victorian dreamer, and his subjects range across the aesthetic spectrum, from classical, biblical and historical to Keats, Tennyson and Boccaccio. His genius lay in the poetic and imaginative way he reinterpreted these familiar subjects. For Waterhouse was very much more of a realist than either Leighton or Burne-Jones. His work shares much of their nostalgia and melancholy, but Waterhouse's nymphs and goddesses are real flesh and blood people, whereas Burne-Jones's figures are like beings from another planet. Looking at 'Hylas and the Nymphs', Waterhouse's most famous picture, we seem to have chanced upon a group of Victorian mermaids in a very English lily pond in the middle of a forest. It is a subject which in the hands of a lesser artist could easily become trite or ridiculous; the key to Waterhouse's style was his gift for combining realism and poetry.

In all Waterhouse's pictures the same romantic, dreamy mood prevails (Colour Plate 16). Once he had found his style, Waterhouse stuck to it for the rest of his career. He may have had only one song to sing, but he sang it very beautifully. During the 1880s and 1890s, his reputation rivalled even that of Leighton and Burne-Jones, and he became an RA in 1895. One of his first successes was the wonderful 'The Lady of Shalott' of 1888. Here Waterhouse combines a favourite Pre-Raphaelite subject with a strongly realistic style, reminiscent of the naturalism of the Newlyn School painters. Waterhouse was friendly with several of the Newlyn artists, such as Frank Bramley, but he never seemed to show any inclination for painting Cornish fisherfolk. He remained faithful to romantic and poetic subjects, particularly those involving the *female fatale*. From the 1890s onwards, all his pictures are of women; men appear only as victims. Typical of Waterhouse is his 'La Belle Dame Sans Merci' of 1893, in which a typical Waterhouse enchantress gently draws the armour-clad knight into her fatal embrace in the middle of a dark and mysterious wood. Waterhouse's Circes and Sirens are not the destructive monsters of Symbolism and Art Nouveau; rather they seem to lure and entrap their victims by their wistful beauty and mysterious sadness, as if they cannot help it.

During the 1890s, Waterhouse's creative genius reached its peak, and this was to be the decade of some of his greatest works, such as 'Ulysses and the Sirens', 'Hylas and the Nymphs', 'Ophelia' and 'St. Cecilia'. After 1900 he turned increasingly to classical subjects, particularly the story of Psyche. His style became more refined in its deliberate sweetness and elegance, but never lapsed into sentimentality or cheap titillation, as it did with so many of his Edwardian contemporaries. He continued to exhibit at the Academy right up to the First War, and remained one of the few respected exponents of the late Pre-Raphaelite style. Unlike so many of his contemporaries, he was a quiet, modest man, who never sought worldly honours, and as a result virtually nothing is known of his private life or his artistic beliefs. No letters or diaries survive but in spite of this Waterhouse's reputation rests secure in the paintings themselves.

The Last Romantics 1890-1920

In 1899 Percy Bate published *The English Pre-Raphaelite Painters,* and it seemed to him that the Pre-Raphaelite movement was still "sweeping on", but that it was "more diffuse". Pre-Raphaelitism was still a noble ideal, but was becoming a vague and loose term, applied to any painting of a romantic or medieval subject, or *femme fatale* with red hair. It could still attract followers, both old and young, but by the early 1900s it was becoming *passé*. The New English Art Club, founded in 1886, was attracting many of the brightest young artists to the Impressionist cause, while the more English-minded ones preferred to paint in Newlyn.

Waterhouse was not the only artist to remain faithful to the Pre-Raphaelite cause. Another was Herbert James Draper, still a largely forgotten and underrated figure, known only for his 'The Lament for Icarus'. Better-known today is John Liston Byam Shaw, who developed a very personal and stylised Pre-Raphaelite manner in the 1890s. Shaw was a great admirer of Rossetti, but painted Rossettian subjects in a brilliant technique more akin to Frederick Sandys. He was also a prolific book illustrator.

As we have seen, the late nineteenth century was a golden age of the illustrated book, especially children's books, and many Pre-Raphaelite artists contributed to this. Through the work of such illustrators as Walter Crane, Henry Justice Ford, Edmund Dulac and Arthur Rackham, Pre-Raphaelite influence was widely disseminated, and continues to influence book illustration today. Another of the many painter-illustrators of this period was Eleanor Fortescue-Brickdale, although more notorious was the short-lived Aubrey Beardsley, who was introduced to Burne-Jones by Oscar Wilde. As a result, Beardsley was commissioned to illustrate a new edition of the *Morte d'Arthur.* The resulting illustrations, which horrified poor Burne-Jones, added a streak of *fin de siècle* decadence and sensuality to the Pre-Raphaelite style, and attracted outrage and admiration in equal measure.

Many late Pre-Raphaelite artists, such as Byam Shaw and Fortescue-Brickdale, continued the Burne-Jones tradition of involvement in decoration and design work. Through the Arts and Crafts Movement, and its many Guilds and Associations, this aspect of Pre-Raphaelitism was kept very much alive. One city with a particularly strong tradition was Birmingham, birthplace of Burne-Jones. Here Joseph Southall, Charles Gere, Arthur Gaskin, Henry Payne, Frederick Cayley Robinson, and other members of the Tempera Society fostered twin Pre-Raphaelite ideals of romantic subjects allied to skilled craftsmanship.

Bate detected Pre-Raphaelite influence in the work of many other painters working in 1899, some of them totally forgotten today. Edward Reginald Frampton and Thomas Cooper Gotch are two who are appreciated today, Frampton for his highly mannered and flowing Art Nouveau style, and Gotch for his elaborate and hieratic

Colour Plate 16. **JOHN WILLIAM WATERHOUSE.** Pandora

pictures which blend Pre-Raphaelitism and the Italian Renaissance. Almost the last of the Pre-Raphaelites was Frank Cadogan Cowper, whose 'Belle Dame Sans Merci' was painted as late as 1926. It is a romantic, Keatsian vision, recalling Waterhouse, Burne-Jones, and even the very earliest days of the Brotherhood, and demonstrates perfectly just how persuasive Pre-Raphaelite ideals were, well into the twentieth century.

Olympian Dreamers — the Classical Movement

Running parallel with the later Pre-Raphaelites was the classical revival, which began in the 1860s as a reaction against the dominance of Ruskin and Pre-Raphaelite ideas, and continued up to 1914. Inevitably these two movements are at times difficult to disentangle, and some artists, such as Albert Moore, Burne-Jones or Waterhouse, managed to keep a foot in both aesthetic camps. Fundamentally, both movements should be considered as branches of the Aesthetic Movement. They are part and parcel of that extraordinary and complex group, the High Victorians. They were all at heart romantics, and in the last resort it mattered little whether you were dreaming of Avalon or Parnassus.

It is however possible to trace a distinct classical movement, particularly in the careers of four artists — Leighton, Watts, Alma-Tadema and Poynter. Through these four, very different Olympians one can see just how the classical ideal influenced Victorian art and culture for over fifty years. Like most classical movements, the Victorian classical revival tells us a great deal more about Victorian England than it does about ancient Greece and Rome. Since the Renaissance, every generation of European artists has sought to reinterpret the great events of classical history and mythology, and the Victorians were no exception. Admiration for Greek and Roman achievements were at the heart of Victorian culture and education.

The Victorian classical revival has very little connection with the Greek revival of the later eighteenth century. By the early Victorian period, the tradition of grand historical painting was faltering, kept alive by a few individualists, such as Daniel Maclise (Colour Plate 18), William Dyce and William Etty. The competition for the decoration of Houses of Parliament gave some of these artists their opportunity, but the suicide of Benjamin Robert Haydon in 1846 was symbolic of the movement's decline. Apart from G.F. Watts, who had studied in Italy and briefly met Haydon, the Victorian classical painters were a completely new and distinct group. In general, their aim was to escape the moral strait-jacket of Ruskin, and the John Bull-ish insularity of the Pre-Raphaelites, and renew contact with the great traditions of European art. They were guided by two main inspirations — Greek sculpture and the Italian Renaissance. A great deal of antique sculpture, including the Elgin marbles, could be seen at the British Museum, and admiration for Greek sculpture is the one common bond that unites nearly all the Victorian classicists. It is also important to remember that the late nineteenth century saw the rediscovery of the Italian Renaissance; this was the Renaissance of the Renaissance. In trying to create

Colour Plate 17. **FREDERIC LEIGHTON.** Invocation

a classical language of their own, the Victorians inevitably looked back to the great heroes of the Renaissance — Michelangelo, Raphael, Leonardo, Titian, Veronese, Botticelli. The Victorian vision of antiquity was expressed in the language of the Renaissance.

The Victorian vision was also a deeply romantic one; the artists looked back wistfully to the classical past as a golden age, far greater and nobler than their own. All Victorian classical painting is imbued with a spirit of intense nostalgia for the past. High points of drama and tragedy are usually avoided; artists preferred scenes involving personal unhappiness, especially abandoned or despairing lovers. The Victorians preferred to contemplate or brood on events, rather than to try and depict them. In painting, this characteristic tended to produce a comfortable, armchair sort of classicism, redolent of the studios of Holland Park and St. John's Wood. At worst, it resulted in polite mediocrity; at best, in a number of striking masterpieces, and one or two artists of genius. It also succeeded in bringing back the nude to Victorian art, after its virtual banishment in the mid-Victorian moral ice age. If all classical movements are a search for an ideal world, then what the Victorians found was a very English Parnassus.

Lord Leighton 1830-1896

Frederic Leighton was the Hercules of Victorian classicism. With his extraordinary range of accomplishments, his noble appearance, his superhuman energy, his lofty devotion to high art, and his unique position as President of the Royal Academy and prince of the Victorian art world, he seemed to belong to the world of gods and heroes. Olympian was the adjective most commonly applied to him. Leighton represents the spirit of Victorian Hellenism at its most notable and inspiring — so much so that there could hardly have been a classical movement in England without him.

Leighton's conversion to classical subjects took place in the 1860s, and it was the Greeks to whom he was attracted. He described the Parthenon as "the greatest architectural emotion of my life, by far", and had a copy of the Parthenon frieze set into his studio walls. He wrote that he was "passionate for the true Hellenic art", and dreamed of making England a new Athens. He wanted to preside over a new Periclean age of the arts, worthy to complement England's position as an imperial power.

Unlike most English artists, Leighton was trained almost entirely on the Continent. As a result, his own art is an extremely complex fusion between European and English influences; a personal combination of Renaissance and classical traditions, overlaid with a sensibility and a colour sense that are entirely Victorian. His first great success came in 1855, when he sent to the Academy a large processional picture entitled 'Cimabue's Celebrated Madonna Carried in Procession through the Streets of Florence'. This type of historical picture involving the life of a famous artist was already very popular in Europe, but was relatively new in England. It was bought by Prince Albert and Queen Victoria for the Royal Collection, and thus Leighton's career was launched.

Leighton finally settled in London in 1859, and at first was unable to repeat the success of 'Cimabue'. His first English pictures were mostly historical or religious, and it was only gradually that he began to move towards classical subjects. In 1865-6 he painted his first major classical work, another processional scene, entitled 'The Syracusan Bride Leading the Wild Beasts to the Temple of Diana'. It is a large, magnificently decorative picture, and shows Leighton moving from the lively and gothic style of 'Cimabue' towards a more classical atmosphere of repose and beauty. As a composition it is rather static, and lacks positive emotion, both characteristic of Leighton's work at this period. His first classical picture to show real drama was the remarkable 'Hercules Wrestling with Death for the Body of Alcestis' painted between 1869 and 1871. During the 1870s he produced two more major works, 'The Daphnephoria', another huge processional picture 17 feet long, and 'Captive Andromache' of 1880, both of which show his classical style finally evolving. But all his greatest works were to be completed towards the end of his life.

It was also during the 1870s that Leighton evolved his more decorative style, typified by such pictures as 'Winding the Skein' or 'Greek Girls Playing at Ball'. These pictures make no attempt at classical drama, or a specific story, and what they may lack in tension, they amply make up for in colour and beauty of composition and outline. It was also at this period that Leighton developed the picture of the single, brooding female figure, that was to become such a hallmark of his style. Outstanding among these were 'Nausicaa', 'The Last Watch of Hero', 'Solitude', or 'Lachrymae' but there were many others (Colour Plate 17). Leighton was also not above producing many charming heads of girls and children, which kept the pot boiling while he was engaged on more major projects.

In 1868, the Royal Academy finally elected Leighton a member. Only ten years later, in 1878, he became President. For the next eighteen years he was to devote himself tirelessly to the affairs of the Academy and the art world. Unlike most artists, Leighton was extremely good at administration and committee work. Under his leadership, the Academy was to enjoy a golden age, attaining levels of prestige, power and prosperity that it has never equalled since. The Academy exhibitions and the Academy Banquet were among the great social occasions of the year, and in 1879 over 400,000 people visited the summer exhibition. By this time, Leighton also felt confident enough to undertake the building of a house. The creation of a house was an important matter for a successful Victorian artist. For Leighton it was not only a space to work in, but also a backdrop for his artistic and worldly ambitions. Over the years he was to pour an immense amount of time, trouble and expense into it, and it is in many ways his most remarkable creation. At one end, he added its most extraordinary feature — the Arab Hall, based on the Moslem palace of La Zisa in Palermo. In its heyday, and especially when Leighton was giving one of his musical evenings, it must have seemed an amazingly sumptuous and impressive building. No house conveys better the life of a high Victorian aesthete and successful establishment artist, and fortunately it is now preserved as a museum.

Unlike most artists, Leighton was one of those who seemed to get better as he got older. Almost all his best works were painted in the last decade of his life. Part of the explanation for this may have been the influence of his greatest muse and model, an actress called Dorothy Dene. She modelled for almost every one of his major works in the 1890s, including 'The Return of Persephone', 'The Bath of

Colour Plate 18. **DANIEL MACLISE.** King Cophetua and the Beggar Maid

Psyche', 'The Garden of the Hesperides', and most famous of all 'Flaming June'. In all these pictures one can detect a new degree of warmth and sensuality, particularly in the lush and vibrant colours. This new element of intensity is what makes these late pictures so remarkable. In January 1896 came the greatest accolade of Leighton's career — a peerage. He is still the only English artist ever to receive this honour. Sadly, he did not live long to enjoy it, as he died only a few weeks later. "Give my love to the Royal Academy", were reportedly his last words; they may be apocryphal, but they seem so fitting an epitaph that it has endured ever since.

George Frederic Watts 1817-1904

Watts was revered by many Victorian artists, Leighton and Burne-Jones included, as a kind of father-figure. As a student, Watts had met Haydon; he had won prizes in the Westminster Hall Competitions; he had spent many years studying in Italy, and was an early admirer of Italian Renaissance painting and Greek sculpture. Alone and neglected, he had struggled to keep alive the tradition of grand historical art in an unsympathetic England. More than any of the other Olympians, Watts was an arch-romantic and an arch-dreamer. He dreamed of reviving great and noble art in England — "raising art to the level it attained in the great days of Greece." He planned huge canvases and vast frescoes. If nobility and high

Colour Plate 19. **GEORGE FREDERIC WATTS.** Hope

intentions were enough to make a great artist, then Watts would certainly have been one. Watts was also a typically high-minded Victorian; religious, but only in a vague, theistic way; but believing devoutly that art had a high mission to improve the lot of mankind. In the 1850s, he had himself photographed, both as a monk holding a bible, and as a knight in chain-mail — a typically Victorian duality.

As a painter, Watts cannot be called a classicist in the narrow sense of the word. Very few of his pictures are of classical subjects, but equally any list of the Victorian Olympians would be incomplete without him. "I paint ideas, not things", claimed Watts, though a Spy cartoon of him was captioned sarcastically "Paints portraits, and ideas". Most of his pictures are allegories, inhabiting a lofty but very Victorian universe, full of vague abstractions such as birth and death, love and life, riches and poverty, good and evil. Watts's seriousness, combined with a murky technique, have combined to make him, until recently, one of the most neglected and misunderstood of all Victorian artists.

Watts was born in London in 1817, the delicate son of a failed piano maker. At a young age he decided to become an artist, and entered the Royal Academy schools in 1835. In 1843 his picture of 'Caractacus' won a prize in the Westminster Competitions, and he decided to use the money to visit Italy. He remained there for three years, from 1844 to 1847, and this was to be the greatest artistic experience of his life. Typically, it was Michelangelo who made the biggest impression on him. In Florence, Watts stayed with the British Minister, Lord Holland, and his vivacious wife Augusta. Here he first began to paint portraits, mainly of Lady Holland and her friends. Watts was later to become one of the greatest Victorian portrait painters, but he always maintained an equivocal, rather priggish attitude to portrait painting that was entirely typical of him. He said that painting portraits made him feel like a shopkeeper, though he undoubtedly found the income useful.

In 1847, Watts returned to London, and won another prize for 'Alfred Inciting the Saxons to Resist the Landings of the Danes', a large and gloomy work which now reposes in a committee room in the Houses of Parliament. But these successes did not lead to the commissions he had hoped for, and the next few years were to be difficult and depressing for him. It was at this period he painted a small group of social realist pictures, such as 'Found Drowned', showing a girl washed ashore under London Bridge. Watts was rescued, as so often in his life, by a masterful woman, Mrs. Sarah Prinsep, a sister of the photographer Julia Margaret Cameron. In 1851, he moved in to the Prinsep's house, Little Holland House, in Holland Park, intending to stay a few days; he was to live there for the next thirty years. Little Holland House had a reputation for bohemianism, and artiness, and was therefore shunned by the respectable. Members of the circle included Ruskin, Tennyson, Thackeray, Dickens, Browning, Leighton, Rossetti, Burne-Jones — anyone who was anyone in mid-Victorian artistic circles. Rossetti took the young Burne-Jones there in 1857, telling him "You must know these people, Ned . . . you will see a painter there, he paints a queer sort of picture about God and Creation." Against this artistic, but secure, background, Watts was able to develop his art in his own very personal way.

In the 1850s Watts received some commissions for frescoes, but he soon realised the difficulties of painting on plaster in the English climate, and turned to painting on canvas instead. His picture of 'Sir Galahad', painted in the late 1850s, was his only concession to Pre-Raphaelitism. His ideas were still classical at this stage, and during the 1860s he painted a number of classical subjects, such as 'The Wife of Pygmalion', based on a supposedly Greek bust in the Ashmolean Museum. He also painted classical nudes, such as 'Thetis', thus giving a lead to Leighton and Albert Joseph Moore. Watts's credo was the form of Phidias and the colour of Titian; lofty, rather nebulous ideals, but typical of the way Victorian artists looked at antiquity with the eyes of the Italian Renaissance (Colour Plate 19). Watts also began his celebrated 'Hall of Fame' series of portraits at this period; Gladstone and Tennyson were among his first sitters.

One myth that particularly appealed to nineteenth century artists was that of 'Orpheus and Eurydice'. Watts painted the subject many times, varying the poses of the figures, and chose the moment when Orpheus turns to look back at Eurydice, thus causing her to sink back into Hades, from whence he had rescued her. Almost his last specifically classical subject was 'Ariadne on Naxos' of 1895. By 1870 he was working on the first of his purely allegorical subjects, 'Love and Death'. This was a subject that so preoccupied Watts that he painted numerous versions of it, some of which were left unfinished at his death. His technique was to sketch in a picture, then turn it to the wall and forget about it, often for as long as twenty or thirty years. It was a technique also used by his beloved Titian, and it has therefore made dating both their pictures extremely difficult. Other compositions of which he produced many versions were 'Love and Life', 'Time, Death and Judgement', and 'The Court of Death'.

In 1872 Watts had to leave Little Holland House, and he then built himself a house and studio in nearby Melbury Road. Holland Park was already something of an artistic colony, with Leighton round the corner, and Val Prinsep, Hamo Thornycroft, Luke Fildes and William Burges further up the road. Next door to Watts in Melbury road lived Mrs. Russell Barrington, described by one biographer as "an indefatigable hunter of artistic big game". She and her husband helped to look after Watts's affairs until 1886, when he married the 36-year old Mary Fraser Tytler. Anxious to move her husband away from Melbury Road, Mrs. Watts decided to build a new house and studio, Limnerslease, at Compton in Surrey. It is this building which now houses the Watts Museum and Art Gallery.

Success finally came to Watts, late in life, but not too late for him to be accepted into the pantheon of Victorian heroes. In 1877 he had a whole room to himself at the Grosvenor Gallery, and in 1881, a one-man show. The Victorians realised they had a grand old man in their midst. His later work is very uneven, but some of his best images, such as 'Mammon', 'For He had Great Possessions', 'The Dweller in the Innermost' and 'The Recording Angel', are extraordinarily effective and powerful. He is at his best in those few canvases, such as 'Chaos' or 'The Sower of the Systems', where his style dissolves into almost complete abstract expressionism. As G.K. Chesterton wrote in his book on Watts, there is a sense of "prehistoric wonder" and "primeval vagueness" about these pictures that comes very close to the cosmic feelings that Watts had been trying all his life to express. Watts invented an artistic language all his own, and deserves to be remembered as one of the great originals of English nineteenth century art.

Sir Lawrence Alma-Tadema 1836-1912

Alma-Tadema is probably the best-known of all the Victorian classical painters, yet he is very much the odd man out. He was Dutch, not English, and only settled in England in 1870, by which time his artistic personality was already fully formed. His character, his temperament, and his art remained, to the end of his life, essentially Dutch.

The contrast between the art of Alma-Tadema and that of Leighton or Watts could hardly be greater. Whereas Leighton and Watts sought to reinterpret the Greek legends of antiquity, Alma-Tadema was concerned to depict daily life in ancient Rome, with the greatest possible degree of accuracy and detail. He was the perfect type of nineteenth century artist-antiquarian. The art of Leighton and Watts is noble, inspirational, intellectual; Alma-Tadema's is real, anecdotal, and down-to-earth. It was said of him that he made antiquity as bourgeois as a Dutch kitchen. The real key to his success was that he made antiquity comprehensible to the Victorian middle classes (Colour Plate 20).

Alma-Tadema entered the Antwerp Academy in 1852, and his early teachers were all historical painters. His own first efforts were mostly obscure scenes from Merovingian or Egyptian history. In 1863 he married his first wife Pauline, and on their honeymoon they visited Italy. Alma-Tadema was doubtless impressed by the grandeur of ancient Rome, but what really fascinated him most were the relics of everyday life he saw at Pompeii and Herculaneum. It was a passion that was to change the direction of his art, and his life. As soon as he returned to Antwerp, he began to paint Roman scenes. At about this time he also met the great dealer Ernest Gambart, the Duveen of the Victorian age, with whom he signed a contract. From that moment, his career was made.

Alma-Tadema kept very precise records, and numbered every picture with Roman numerals. We know that between 1865 and 1870 he painted forty-five classical subjects, and was encouraged towards this type of picture by Gambart. This is known as his Pompeian period, because of his love of ornate interiors with walls of rich Pompeian red. Already Alma-Tadema was showing a mastery of technique which few of his contemporaries could rival. He also painted two specifically Greek subjects at this time, 'Phidias and the Parthenon' and 'A Pyrrhic Dance'. In 1869, his first wife died, and in 1870 he decided to settle in London, where Gambart had already had considerable success in selling his pictures. The classical revival was beginning to gather momentum, and Alma-Tadema proved to be the right man, in the right place, at the right time. His success was not with the intelligensia, who generally disliked his work, but with the Victorian *nouveaux riches*. They appreciated his pictures because they combined realistic detail, anecdotal content, and a modicum of classical culture, something in which they may have felt themselves to be deficient.

The 1870s and 1880s were to be tremendously busy and productive years; in 1874 alone he produced twenty-one finished pictures. Alma-Tadema was quickly

Colour Plate 20. **LAWRENCE ALMA-TADEMA.** The Colosseum

accepted into the establishment; in 1876 he became an ARA and in 1879 a full RA. His finest works of this period were his Roman spectaculars, such as 'Antony and Cleopatra', and 'The Roses of Heliogabalus', or Greek subjects such as 'A Dedication to Bacchus' or 'The Women of Amphissa'. In these works, all traces of his early Belgian heaviness have disappeared. Thanks to the influence of Leighton and Albert Joseph Moore, his colours became lighter, and his figures more attractive. Alma-Tadema was also influenced, like them, by Japanese art, not only in his use of more delicate colours, but also in his use of deliberately abrupt and striking perspectives. His use of such techniques as cutting off heads and bodies at the edge of a picture, or creating vertiginous drops, made a great impression on the Victorian public. Pictures like 'The Kiss' or 'The Coign of Vantage' also show Alma-Tadema's awareness of photography. Like Degas, he was much interested in the pioneering work of Edward Muybridge, the first photographer to attempt motion pictures.

During the 1880s, Alma-Tadema's career went from strength to strength. In 1882 he was accorded the honour of a one-man exhibition at the Grosvenor Gallery. He was also very involved with theatrical design. In 1885 he and his second wife, Laura, herself a very talented painter, moved to a new large house in St. John's Wood. After lavish alterations, this was to become one of London's best-known artistic houses, and a popular location for weekly At Homes, concerts and parties. Alma-Tadema was a genial host, and very popular among his fellow-artists, who gave a great dinner in his honour when he received a knighthood in 1899.

In the 1890s his prodigious output began to slow down, but he was still capable of very good things, particularly scenes of Roman baths, such as 'The Frigidarium', 'A Favourite Custom', and the spectacular 'Baths of Caracalla'. As he grew older, Alma-Tadema began to simplify his pictures, reducing them to a figure, or groups of figures, on a marble bench by the sea, with flowers to add a note of colour. As celebrations of sea, sky, marble and flowers, bathed in Mediterranean sunshine, these pictures are unique in Victorian art. This was a type of picture endlessly imitated by Alma-Tadema's many followers, one of the more competent being John William Godward who developed his own very personal variation of the theme (Colour Plate 21).

Alma-Tadema lived on into the twentieth century, but the fashion for his pictures was beginning to wane. After his death in 1912, taste had already begun to move away from Victorian art. Yet when the other Olympians were forgotten, Alma-Tadema always remained notorious. The critics of the 1920s and 1930s loved to single him out as the supreme example of Victorian bad taste. Ironically, his influence lived on in the cinema, especially in the films of D.W. Griffiths and Cecil B. de Mille, both of whom admired his work. Now, Alma-Tadema's pictures are as popular as ever, and he is restored to his rightful place in the Victorian pantheon.

Sir Edward John Poynter 1836-1919
Poynter remains the least known and the least appreciated of the Olympians. And yet he was Leighton's chief disciple and follower; after Leighton's death it was Poynter who assumed his toga as leader of the Classical Movement, becoming President of the Academy in 1896, a post which he was to hold for twenty-two

years. Poynter's personality and his artistic achievements have always been overshadowed by those of Leighton. He also lived too long. His reign as PRA was to see the complete overthrow of all the artistic values in which he had believed since youth. Poynter's reaction was to turn his face against all modern movements in art, and doggedly to continue painting classical maidens on marble terraces. It was heroic, but also slightly ridiculous.

Poynter met Leighton in Rome in 1853, and immediately fell under his spell. Returning to London, he studied briefly at various schools, but decided in 1855 to move to Paris. There he enrolled in the studio of Charles Gleyre, a pupil of Ingres, and was soon imbibing the heady atmosphere of heroic and romantic classicism that prevailed in Paris at the time. For a time Poynter shared rooms with the youthful Whistler, and later with three English students, Thomas Reynolds Lamont, Thomas Armstrong, and George Du Maurier. Later they were all to be immortalised in Du Maurier's hugely successful novel *Trilby*.

Returning to London in 1859, Poynter became involved, like many young and struggling artists, in design and illustration work. He also worked briefly for the arch-goth architect, William Burges. In 1865 he achieved his first, much-needed, success with 'Faithful Unto Death', depicting a Roman soldier remaining at his post during the destruction of Pompeii. Poynter's formula was to combine historical accuracy with heroic action, and he was to repeat it in 1867 with 'Israel in Egypt', and in 1868 with 'The Catapult' (Plate 7). These successes led to his election as an ARA in 1869, and during the 1870s he was to become increasingly involved in teaching and administration. Poynter was a natural candidate for posts of this kind, not only because he was a reliable and sober individual, but also because of his strict adherence to academic principles. This was the strength, as well as the weakness, of Poynter's art.

During the 1870s he also received his largest private commission, to decorate the

Colour Plate 21
JOHN WILLIAM GODWARD .
Absence Makes the Heart Grow
Fonder

billiard room at Wortley Hall, near Sheffield, for the Earl of Wharncliffe. This
involved four large compositions, three classical, and one medieval. Regrettably, all
these pictures have since been destroyed, leaving a major gap in Poynter's *oeuvre*.
Pictures which do survive, such as 'A Visit to Aesculapius' and 'Horae Serenae',
show his idealistic vision of antiquity. In contrast to the dramatic and restless late
works of Leighton, Poynter's pictures are bland, serene and restful. In his dream
world, laughing and beautiful girls do nothing all day but dance, swim and chatter
under blue skies, in completely correct, yet chaste, classical attitudes (Colour Plate
22). It is a Victorian schoolmaster's vision of antiquity.

After 1900, Poynter's work becomes increasingly decorative, and much influenced
by the style of his successful rival, Alma-Tadema. He was still capable, however, of
the occasional surprise, such as the magnificently decorative 'Cave of the Storm
Nymphs' of 1903. As his creative powers began to wane, honours were increasingly
showered upon him; in 1902 he was made a baronet. He was fortunate in his choice
of wife, Agnes, one of the four beautiful and dynamic MacDonald sisters, all of
whom made remarkable marriages. Georgiana married Burne-Jones, Alice married

Colour Plate 22. **EDWARD JOHN POYNTER.** A Roman Boat Race

John Kipling, father of Rudyard Kipling, and Louie married Alfred Baldwin, father of Stanley Baldwin, later Prime Minister. Sadly Agnes Poynter died in 1906, and thereafter Poynter became increasingly withdrawn and uncommunicative. The artistic world was changing, but he refused to change with it. His answer to Post-Impressionism, Cubism, Fauvism, the aeroplane, the cinema, and the twentieth century, was to ignore them. He remained faithful to the old gods. Like the Roman soldier in his first successful picture, he too was 'Faithful Unto Death'.

Albert Joseph Moore 1841-1893 and the Aesthetic Parnassus

Both the Classical and Aesthetic Movements first took root in the 1860s, and from the start they ran parallel. Leighton was to emerge as leader of the classical school, and Burne-Jones of the aesthetic, but it is more or less impossible to say where classicism ends and aestheticism begins. They frequently meet in the personalities of some artists, such as Albert Moore, Simeon Solomon, and above all, Burne-Jones himself, who frequently painted classical subjects. It is perhaps best to see the Classical Movement as part of the larger Aesthetic Movement. Even Leighton himself, although he preferred classical subjects, was a typical high Victorian aesthete. For many Victorian artists, such as Waterhouse, the only difference between Parnassus and Camelot was a choice of subject matter. The Classical Movement, the later Pre-Raphaelites, and the Aesthetic Movement should all be seen as interrelated and complementary, part of that rich and complex tapestry that is High Victorian art.

The Grosvenor Gallery, founded in 1877, became the focal point of the Aesthetic Movement, and tended to attract more progressive artists. Leighton became President of the RA in 1878, but even he was not above showing at the Grosvenor occasionally. An atmosphere of tolerance and cameraderie seemed to prevail in High Victorian art circles. Artistic battles were fought out in the columns of *Punch*, where everyone could enjoy George Du Maurier's cartoons lampooning the aesthetes of Passionate Brompton. At the Grosvenor, unlike the Academy, the pictures were well spaced apart, with groups of one artist's work hanging together. Among the artists whose work was shown in this way were Burne-Jones, Watts, Whistler, Tissot and Albert Moore.

In the work of Albert Moore, the Classical and Aesthetic Movements meet. Moore was a close friend of Whistler between 1865 and 1870, and is therefore an important figure in the development of the Aesthetic Movement. Moore believed, like Whistler, that beauty, colour, harmony and line were all that mattered in painting. But Moore was also a great admirer of Greek sculpture, especially the Elgin marbles, and most of his pictures are of girls in vaguely classical robes (Colour Plate 23). This had led to Moore being labelled a classicist, but this is a superficial definition. Unlike Alma-Tadema or Poynter, Moore was not remotely interested in historical or archaeological accuracy. Unlike Leighton, he was not concerned with classical myth, or with depicting drama or passion. Also unlike most of the other Olympians, Moore was a shy and retiring bachelor, who lived in complete bohemian disorder in a studio in Holland Park full of cats. He made no effort whatever to pursue either wealth or worldly honours. Above all he was interested in colour; he was one of the outstanding colourists of English art, and his true

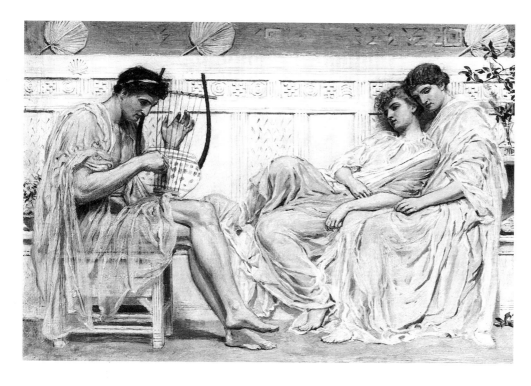

greatness is only now beginning to be recognised.

Like many young artists of the 1860s, Moore studied at the Royal Academy Schools, and in France and Italy. Like Poynter, he also became involved in decorative work. His first exhibits at the Royal Academy were of girls in classical robes. In 1866 he painted 'Pomegranates', which shows his style changing radically. The picture simply shows three girls grouped round a cabinet decorated with geometric patterns. Other accessories are deliberately introduced for their effects of colour, and the whole picture has a two-dimensional flatness. One can already detect the influence of Whistler. Moore introduced Whistler to classical sculpture, and Whistler indoctrinated Moore with his aesthetic principles, and also introduced him to Japanese art. This was to have the effect of making Moore's colours lighter and more delicate, and his pictures more concerned with all-over decorative effects. 'A Musician' of circa 1867 shows how Moore was able to reconcile the arts of Japan and Greece in a new Victorian combination (Plate 8). About this time both Whistler and Moore began to use devices as signatures, Whistler a butterfly, Moore a Greek anthemion.

By the mid-1870s, Moore's style had evolved. For twenty years he continued to perfect it, refine it, elaborate it, but not change it. He exhibited on average one large picture a year, usually at the RA. His pictures fall into two types, single standing or reclining female figures, or frieze-like groups of three or four figures. At their best, these pictures achieve a simplicity of design and delicacy of colour quite unique in Victorian art. It says much for the strength of Victorian patronage that Moore, in spite of his reclusive nature, never lacked patrons or admirers. To get the effects he wanted, he built up an extraordinarily elaborate and academic technique, beginning with cartoons, studies of the figure, nude and draped, and drapery studies, and going on to five different stages of painting. It was this technique that accounts for the very light key of Moore's pictures, and their luminosity, as if one was looking through a thin gauze veil. So great was Moore's preoccupation with colour that he often repeated a composition, such as 'Apples', using a different colour scheme. And

Colour Plate 23. **ALBERT JOSEPH MOORE.** A Revery

so uninterested was he in narrative content that he often refused to give his pictures titles, saying to the patron, "call it what you like". Inevitably this has led to Moore being compared with abstract colourists of the twentieth century, but at heart he was essentially a Victorian and Olympian figure. Although a great innovator in some ways, he was deeply classical and conservative in others.

Classical and aesthetic influences also combine in the work of many artists who are usually labelled as Pre-Raphaelites, particularly Burne-Jones, Simeon Solomon, and J.W. Waterhouse, all of whom have already been mentioned. Burne-Jones's mature style is a particularly complex and personal fusion between Pre-Raphaelitism, the Italian Renaissance, and classicism. During the 1860s and 1870s he painted a number of classical subjects, such as 'The Pygmalion Series', 'Phyllis and Demophoön', and 'Venus Epithalamia'. The model for several of these pictures was his mistress, the beautiful Greek sculpt. uress, Maria Zambaco. For Burne-Jones, this striking Greek girl must have represented a living embodiment of the classical ideal he was searching for. Although Burne-Jones gradually abandoned classical subjects as he got older, some of his greatest works, such as 'The Mirror of Venus' (Plate 6) and the 'Perseus' series are based on classical legend. Many of Burne Jones's ideas were based on William Morris's poem *The Earthly Paradise*, a long Chaucerian poem in which classical and medieval legends are mixed together. This shows just what a complex, hybrid brand of classicism Burne-Jones's was, filtered through the distorting mirrors of the Middle Ages and the Renaissance. Like all great artists, Burne-Jones had extraordinary powers of assimilation, and his art is virtually a microcosm of all the varying ideas and influences that go to make up High Victorian art. A similar mixture of aestheticism and classicism can be found in many of Burne-Jones's followers, in particular Walter Crane, Evelyn De Morgan, J.R. Spencer-Stanhope, J.M. Strudwick and S.H. Meteyard (Colour Plate 24).

Lesser Olympians 1870-1920
Between 1870 and 1900, the Classical Movement was in full swing. Greek tragedies were revived on the London stage, and Victorian ladies began to wear Athenian tea-gowns. Classical subjects had become a vogue, both among the younger artists wanting to make their name, and among older artists ready to trim their sails to suit the new artistic breezes blowing in from Italy and Greece. Leighton himself encouraged many young artists, but had few actual pupils. One of his more successful protégés was Charles Edward Perugini, who painted a number of highly decorative classical pictures under Leighton's influence. Later he married Kate Dickens, daughter of Charles Dickens. Kate Perugini was also a talented painter, mostly of sentimental pictures of women and children.

Val Prinsep, who helped Rossetti and Burne-Jones with the Oxford Union frescoes, developed into a painter of very diverse talents. Some of his pictures are classical, but like many later Victorian artists, Prinsep strayed beyond Greece and Rome towards the exotic civilisations of the east — Babylonian, Assyrian, Egyptian. Another exponent of this genre was Edwin Long, painter of the 'The Babylonian Marriage Market', which in its day fetched a record price for the work of a living artist.

Sir William Blake Richmond was a disciple of Leighton, and painted a number of large, processional classical subjects, many of which have now been lost or

destroyed. His 'Venus and Anchises' in the Walker Art Gallery, Liverpool, shows what a good painter he could be at his best. Both Solomon Joseph Solomon and The Hon. John Collier exploited the more dramatic side of Greek drama. Several of their best works are in Australian museums, but Collier's 'Clytemnestra' is in the Guildhall Art Gallery in London. Briton Riviere made a speciality of classical subjects involving animals, such as 'Apollo' or 'Dead Hector'. Herbert Draper can be compared with Waterhouse, and like him had a penchant for scenes from Homer. Several lady artists turned with success to classical subjects, in particular Sophie Anderson, Henrietta Rae, and Anna Lea Merritt, painter of the well-known 'Love Locked Out' in the Tate Gallery.

After 1900, the number of classical pictures exhibited at the RA began to decline. Waterhouse was still exhibiting regularly, and there were a few artists who remained faithful to the old gods. Among Alma-Tadema's many followers, the best was John William Godward (Colour Plate 21). He painted only classical maidens on marble terraces, but with a degree of technical mastery and monumentality that at times almost rivals Alma-Tadema or Leighton. Many other 'painters of the patio' repeated the recipe — Henry Ryland, G.L. Bulleid, W. Anstey Dollond and W.S. Coleman among them. Grand classical spectaculars of a rather cinematic type were produced by such artists as T.R. Spence, H.G. Schmalz and Sigismund Goetz. Very little research has yet been done into the links between Victorian painting and the cinema, but the connections are obvious on visual grounds alone. By 1914 classical subjects had died out almost completely, and classicism in painting was becoming a dead language.

Colour Plate 25. **HUBERT von HERKOMER.** Hard Times

Colour Plate 26. **FRANK HOLL.** Deserted

High Life and Low Life — Social Realist Painting in the 1870s and 1880s

During the 1870s and 1880s not all artists were Pre-Raphaelites or followers of the Aesthetic Movement. Many artists continued to find inspiration in scenes of contemporary life. During the 1860s it was Frith and his followers who dominated the modern-life scene, but in the 1870s a group of younger artists began to paint social realist pictures of an altogether more serious type. The three most interesting were Sir Luke Fildes, Frank Holl, and Sir Hubert von Herkomer. All three worked as illustrators for *The Graphic*, an illustrated magazine which concentrated on exposing some of the worst social evils of the age. They were also admirers of the works of Frederick Walker, whose monumental and nostalgic pictures of country people, such as 'The Vagrants' of 1868, attracted huge admiration in the 1860s and 1870s. Sadly, Walker died young in 1875. Another avid reader of *The Graphic* was the young Van Gogh, who lived in London between 1873 and 1876. He retained his admiration for English illustrators to the end, and often referred to Walker, Millais, Holl and Herkomer in his letters.

The first artist to attract notice was Luke Fildes. His large and gloomy picture of 'Applicants for Admission to a Casual Ward' was shown at the RA of 1874, and caused a sensation. Fildes was hailed as 'Hogarth's successor', but many critics complained that the subject matter made it an unsuitable picture for a drawing room. The *Art Journal* in particular was always fiercely critical of social realist pictures. They were even less pleased with Fildes's next picture, entitled 'The Widower'. After this, unfortunately for posterity, Fildes turned to the calmer and more profitable waters of portraiture and fancy pictures of children and girls. Royal commissions, a knighthood, and a large Norman Shaw house in Melbury Road, Holland Park, were his reward. He died, rich and famous, in 1927, but after his celebrated 'The Doctor' of 1891, he never painted another memorable picture.

The career of Hubert von Herkomer followed a very similar pattern. The son of a German woodcarver, he worked as an illustrator in the 1870s and achieved his first success in 1875 with 'The Last Muster, Sunday at the Royal Hospital, Chelsea'. He followed this in 1878 with 'Eventide', a scene in the Westminster Workhouse for Women. It was not until 1885 that he painted another major social realist subject, 'Hard Times' (Colour Plate 25), now his most famous picture. It shows an agricultural labourer, with his wife and two children, 'on the tramp' looking for work, and resting in a country lane. The figures were modelled in the studio from a local labourer and his family, and the heroic pose of the workman strongly recalls Fred Walker, whose work Herkomer admired. The mother with two children is a Victorian version of the Madonna resting on 'The Flight into Egypt'. Although the picture exudes a feeling of suffering and hardship, the purposeful stance of the workman suggests hope and strength, and eventual triumph over adversity. After this Herkomer only painted one or two more realist scenes, such as 'On Strike' of 1890. He, too, was drawn inexorably down the primrose path to fashionable portrait painting. Honours were showered upon him — the CVO, a knighthood, even a German title from the Kaiser. He founded an art school at Bushey, built a monstrous Germanic house called Lululaund, and a Wagnerian tower in Germany, was Slade Professor, wrote operas, lived to design both for the stage and the cinema and died in 1914, a veritable pillar of the art establishment.

Frank Holl was the most interesting of the three, and the best painter, but sadly he died in 1888 aged only forty-three. He too became an outstandingly able and successful portrait painter, but his interest in social realism was more than just a passing phase and he was not afraid of a sad subject (Colour Plate 26). His first successes were mostly scenes of the lives of fisherfolk, such as 'No Tidings from the Sea' of 1870, which was bought by Queen Victoria. Dramas of life by the sea were very popular in the 1870s and 1880s, and the lost boat, the waiting women, the wreck and the lifeboat became the stock-in-trade of many Victorian artists. In search of subjects, Holl prowled the streets of the East End, often at night. Seeing two policeman carrying a foundling baby, he turned this into 'Deserted — A Foundling', exhibited at the RA in 1874. The death of children was for the Victorians a very real and often heart-rending subject, and Holl's painting 'Her Firstborn' of 1876, showing the burial of a young baby, is a genuine and moving cry of anguish. It is one of the most moving pictures of a child's funeral ever painted. The *Art Journal* wrote: "Mr Holl, we are sure, never painted better, or made the onlooker sadder." Pictures of funerals and graveyards were intensely emotive subjects for the Victorians.

Visiting Newgate Prison, Holl witnessed another scene that was to result in his most famous picture, 'Newgate — Committed for Trial'. This shows a wife and her children visiting her husband, a bank clerk who had cheated his employees and had been sentenced to five years' penal servitude. This is one of the masterpieces of English social realism. As a movement, social realism did not last. The critics were hostile, and the English buying public were not sympathetic to this type of picture. English artists were fettered by the bias towards narrative, the need to make every picture tell a story. This led to endless pictures of widows, such as Millais's 'Widow's Mite', or Emily Mary Osborn's 'Nameless and Friendless', a Victorian classic of the forlorn widow trying to make ends meet by selling her own pictures. Only occasionally did English art produce a realistic, honest picture of ordinary Victorian life, such as 'The Public Bar' by John Henry Henshall, or 'The Dinner Hour, Wigan' by Eyre Crowe.

Much more to the public taste were pictures of high life. Surprisingly, the greatest painter of English social life in the Victorian period was not English, but French — Jacques Joseph Tissot, or James Tissot as he liked to be known. Tissot was a fashionable Parisian painter in the 1860s, and in 1871 he was forced by the Commune risings to flee to London, as were many other artists. He had already worked as a caricaturist for *Vanity Fair* magazine, and painted a superb portrait of one of its founders, 'Colonel Burnaby'. So it was perhaps natural that he should turn to London society as a subject for paintings. His first success at the Royal Academy in 1873 was 'Too Early', showing an embarrassed group of guests who have arrived at a dance too early. He followed this with 'The Ball on Shipboard', and 'Hush', showing guests assembling for a private musical recital. In these pictures Tissot produced a brilliantly adapted French Salon picture to suit Victorian taste, and his work was an instant success. In a very few years he had established himself as a highly popular and prosperous artist, to the astonished envy of his French colleagues, including his friend Degas. Tissot was also drawn to the bustling life of the Thames, and some of his finest pictures are of pretty women on board ship, such as 'The Last Evening', 'The Captain's Daughter', or 'The Captain and the Mate' (Colour Plate 28). Although hugely popular with the public, Tissot's pictures were scorned by the critics, who tended to dismiss them snobbishly as depicting vulgar, overdressed *parvenus*. Elegant though Tissot's pictures are to the twentieth century viewer, it is important to realise that they reflect the self-consciously smart world of the aspiring middle-class, not the aristocracy.

Above all, Tissot was a painter of women. He was obsessed by pretty, elegant women,

Colour Plate 27. **JAMES HAYLLAR.** Ready for the Party

Colour Plate 28. **JAMES TISSOT.** The Captain and the Mate

and no one has painted them with such devotion. About 1876, he met his *femme fatale*, in the shape of a beautiful divorcee called Kathleen Newton. She became his mistress, and moved with her two illegitimate children into Tissot's house in St. John's Wood. From then on, Kathleen became the model for almost all his pictures. She was a typical Tissot beauty — petite, elegant, pretty, and with a sad, wistful expression. The pictures and domestic scenes that Tissot painted of her and her children are among the most delightful of all his works. Sadly Kathleen Newton, like the Victorian heroine she was, died of consumption in 1882, at the age of only 28. Tissot was so distraught at her death that he immediately fled back to Paris, having sold his house to Alma-Tadema. A few years later, he had a religious conversion, and spent the rest of his life illustrating the bible. A strange end for the painter of fashionable society.

Tissot had no real rivals in England, although he made one surprising convert in Atkinson Grimshaw, the painter of moonlit docks and roads. During the 1870s Grimshaw painted a number of aesthetic interiors with women, which show that he must have studied Tissot's pictures at the Grosvenor Gallery. Edward John Gregory's 'Boulter's Lock: Sunday Afternoon' was one of the few English pictures to rival Tissot's elegance. More modest, but equally delightful, are the pictures of the painter James Hayllar and his four daughters. The Hayllar family lived at Castle Priory, Wallingford on Thames, and almost all of their pictures were painted in or around the house (Colour Plate 27). They present us with an absolutely charming insight into the life of a middle-class artistic family. Edith Hayllar's 'A Summer Shower', showing a party of tennis players taking refuge indoors, is perhaps one of the most delightful of all Victorian narrative pictures of modern life.

Portrait Painting

The Victorian period used not generally to be thought of as a great epoch for portrait painting, but this can now be seen to be a myth. After the death of Sir Thomas Lawrence in 1830, the tradition of portraiture in the grand romantic manner did seem to come to an end. But the Victorian period in fact produced an abundance of interesting portrait painters and good portraits, while the later Victorian and Edwardian period was a positive golden age of English portraiture — the age of Sargent, Lavery and Orpen.

The 1840s, it has to be admitted, only produced a moderate crop of portrait painters. George Richmond's many watercolours and oils of this period have a high level of competence and charm, but a tendency to superficiality. Richmond's motto was "the truth lovingly told", and most of his work echoes this sentiment. The Chalon brothers produced work of a similar type, and Margaret Carpenter is best remembered for her series of Eton leaving portraits. John Linnell, in his early years, produced a great number of portraits, some of which are of beautiful quality, but he later gave it up in favour of landscape painting. Although Daniel Maclise also did portraits as a young man, and is chiefly known now for his portrait of Charles Dickens of 1839, his real ambition was to be a history painter. Among Queen Victoria's early court painters were George Hayter and John Partridge, whose work is competent but rarely distinguished. The Queen was also painted, on horseback, by Sir Francis Grant, later President of the Royal Academy, and one of the best of the early Victorian portrait painters. Grant was a hunting man, and one of his best-known pictures was 'The Hunt Breakfast'. He was also popular in society, and a favourite painter among the aristocracy and gentry. His portraits exude an air of distinction and self-confidence, and still hang in many an English country house, looking quite at ease alongside the Reynolds, the Gainsboroughs, or the Lawrences of previous generations. In Scotland, the tradition of grand portraiture established by Ramsay and Raeburn was carried on into the Victorian period by such artists as Sir John Watson Gordon, Andrew Geddes and Daniel Macnee. David Wilkie also occasionally attempted portraits in the grand manner, but this was not an area much suited to his talents.

The marriage of Queen Victoria and Prince Albert opened a new epoch in court portraiture. The first court favourite was Sir Edwin Landseer, who painted several pictures of the royal couple, such as 'Windsor Castle in Modern Times'. Landseer did not regard himself as a portrait painter, and liked to combine portraits with animals or game. He painted many such pictures of the royal family at Balmoral, and was also commissioned by other aristocratic patrons to do the same thing for them. Many of the results were delightful, but Landseer found great difficulty in finishing portraits, and eventually tried to stop painting them altogether. Landseer in his turn was eclipsed by Franz Xaver Winterhalter, the greatest court painter of the nineteenth century who painted royalty and aristocracy all over Europe. Between 1842 and 1871 he visited England almost every summer, and painted more than a hundred works for Victoria and Albert. These range from the grand set-piece royal portraits, to delightful watercolour studies of the royal children. After Albert's death, Victoria still tended to use foreign artists, such as Heinrich von Angeli, much to the chagrin of English painters, who considered that the English royal family should be painted by English artists.

The Pre-Raphaelites, in the early years of the Brotherhood, received few portrait commissions, but they did find time to make numerous drawings of each other. Later many of them were to paint portraits, and they brought to portraiture the same intensity and desire for truth that they sought in their other pictures. Holman Hunt's two portraits of clerics, John David Jenkins, and Henry Wentworth Monk, are both typical of the Pre-Raphaelite approach. Painted close-up, they subject the sitter to a searching scrutiny, and excude an almost tangible intensity. Millais also painted a few portraits in the 1850s, in particular his famous portrait of John Ruskin in Scotland. Although painted under trying circumstances, this is probably the finest of all Pre-Raphaelite portraits, and expresses perfectly the mystical reverence for the minutiae of nature which was the cornerstone of Ruskin's philosophy. Later Millais broadened his style, and became one of the most highly-paid and successful of all Victorian portrait painters. It has been fashionable to dismiss Millais's later work, but some of his best portraits, such as those of Gladstone, Louise Jopling or Kate Perugini, can stand comparison with any portraits of the late Victorian period. Ford Madox Brown's few portraits are characterised by the fearless honesty so typical of him.

Most of Rossetti's most beautiful portraits were drawings, either of Elizabeth Siddal or Jane Morris (Plate 3). He only occasionally painted portraits in watercolour, mostly of close friends. Burne-Jones also painted portraits, but they have an air of ethereal spirituality that makes them seem more like figures in his paintings than actual portraits. His portraits of the beautiful Maria Zambaco are a good example of this. The Pre-Raphaelite follower who made the greatest contribution to portraiture was Frederick Sandys. His portrait oils, particularly of old ladies, such as Mrs. Susannah Rose, or Mrs. Jane Lewis, have a level of technical accomplishment which recalls the pictures of Holbein or Dürer. Later Sandys gave up oils in favour of chalk, and here again his elaborate and highly-wrought portraits in coloured chalks are masterly feats of technique in this difficult medium.

The Grosvenor Gallery saw the development of the aesthetic portrait. Its chief exponent was Whistler, who had already by then painted the famous portraits of his mother and of Thomas Carlyle. He gave both these pictures the title 'Arrangement in Grey and Black', reflecting his insistence on the aesthetic philosophy that colour, line and harmony were the overriding factors in a portrait, just as they were in any of his pictures (Colour Plate 30). Whistler's sense of design, his subtlety of colour, and his ruthless perfectionism led to many beautiful portraits in the 1870s and 1880s, but his quarrelsome temperament also led to disputes with his sitters, most notably with the distinguished amateur Sir William Eden.

Among the classical painters, G.F. Watts was alone in devoting himself to portraiture. From the mid-1850s be began to build up a collection of portraits of famous men of his day, later known as 'The Hall of Fame' collection. Overwhelmingly serious and high-minded, Watts's portraits present us with a unique panorama of the great men of the age. Like many mild and professional types, Watts was a great hero-worshipper. He tried to avoid commissioned portraits, as did Leighton, but both occasionally succumbed, not usually with happy

Colour Plate 29. **JOHN SINGER SARGENT.** Carnation Lily Lily Rose

Colour Plate 30. **JAMES ABBOTT McNEILL WHISTLER** .
The Little White Girl: Symphony in White, No. 2

results. Poynter was more effective as a portrait painter, as was Val Prinsep, both of whom produced some interesting and delightful portraits. Much in demand in the late Victorian period was Sir William Blake Richmond, son of George Richmond. He painted many interesting sitters, such as the Liddell sisters (Alice Liddell was the original Alice in Wonderland), Andrew Lang, and the Princess of Wales.

All three of *The Graphic* artists, Holl, Fildes and Herkomer turned to successful careers as portrait painters. Of the three, the best painter was Frank Holl. His portraits combine penetrating characterisation with a robust and flowing technique, the figures often looming out of the dark, Rembrandtesque background. This can be seen in his portraits of William Agnew, the art dealer, or Earl Spencer, known as the Red Earl. Herkomer was capable of the occasional fine portrait, but much of his work in this direction is worthy but dull. Much the same can be said of Luke Fildes, but some of his portraits of society ladies have great charm and decorative appeal. Another late Victorian and Edwardian artist capable of a good portrait was Sir Frank Dicksee, who eventually became President of the RA very late in life, in 1918, after the death of Poynter. Many other late Victorians occasionally turned to portraiture, including James Guthrie, Alma-Tadema, John Collier, Archibald Stuart Wortley, and others too numerous to mention.

It also has to be remembered that most of the great Edwardian portrait painters — Sargent (Colour Plate 29), Lavery, Orpen, J.J. Shannon to name but a few — were all painting at the end of the Victorian period. One either has to regard them as late Victorians, or early Edwardians. It is in my view more sensible to see the Edwardian period as the final chapter of the Victorian age, and therefore the Victorian age can truly be described as one of the great periods of English portraiture.

Landscape Painting
The English have always particularly appreciated landscape painting, and this was especially true of the Victorians. Landscape was probably the single most popular type of picture in the Victorian period. The Royal Academy exhibitions were dominated by landscapes, and nineteenth century landscapes are still filling salerooms up and down the country every week even now. As with so much else, many of these Victorian landscapes were of mediocre quality, and deliberately prettified to appeal to the taste of the day. But the Victorian period also produced a large number of very good landscape artists. Some, like John Linnell or B.W. Leader, may one day be numbered among our greatest landscape painters. The Pre-Raphaelite movement, as we have already seen, produced some of the finest landscapes in English art, and had an immense influence on landscape painters and watercolourists for the rest of the century.

Turner died in 1851, well into the Victorian period. His late works were regarded as the incomprehensible eccentricities of an old man, but thanks to the support of Ruskin, his reputation remained high throughout the nineteenth century. He also attracted followers and imitators, particularly James Baker Pyne. Another relic of the romantic era was John Martin, who did not die until 1854. In the 1840s he was still painting many beautiful and romantic landscapes. It was also at this late stage in his career that he painted his famous 'Judgement' pictures — 'The Plains of Heaven', 'The Last Judgement' and 'The Great Day of his Wrath', now among the best known pictures in the Tate Gallery. John Constable, the greatest landscape painter of the nineteenth century, died in 1837, the year of Queen Victoria's accession to the throne. His work was neglected for most of the century, but he had some admirers, and one faithful pupil, Frederick William Watts. Constable's work was too rugged, too honest, and too impressionistic to find favour with most Victorian collectors. The Victorians preferred the sentimental rusticity of William Collins, the highly-charged romanticism of Linnell, the gentle lyricism of B.W. Leader, the grand effects of George Vicat Cole or the Pre-Raphaelite intensity of John Brett and William Dyce. What most Victorians wanted, like Mr. Millbank, the industrialist in Disraeli's novel *Coningsby*, was "a fine free landscape by F.R. Lee, that gave him the broad plains, the green lanes, and running streams of his own land."

The Victorians lived in the first industrial age. For them the city, the factory and the railway were new experiences, and this made their nostalgia for the countryside correspondingly intense. The Victorian merchant, in his comfortable suburban villa, wanted a pretty, idealised view of the countryside, peopled with contented and picturesque peasants going about their work or their rustic pleasures. He certainly did not want to know about any of the nasty things going on in the countryside. The list of artists who catered for this insatiable demand for pretty landscapes and peasant girls is endless, and I can only mention a few. In the 1840s the most popular landscape painter was William Collins, whose best-known picture, 'Rustic Civility', shows a rosy-cheeked infant opening a gate to a stranger. William Shayer, one of a Hampshire family of artists, painted attractive scenes, often with gypsies, in the New Forest. He sometimes collaborated with Edward Charles Williams, a member of another artistic tribe, the Williams family. They were so numerous that several of them changed their names, notably Henry John Boddington and Sidney Richard Percy. The Williams family were all prolific and popular artists, exhibiting at the Royal Academy and elsewhere for almost the entire Victorian period. Another artistic dynasty was the Meadows family, which included several landscape painters. River scenes were the speciality of Thomas Creswick, another enormously prolific artist, who exhibited for many years at the Royal Academy, and in due course became a member. John Brandon Smith went one further and developed a speciality of painting waterfalls. Almost anything was possible in the Victorian period.

In a much higher class is the work of Benjamin Williams Leader (Colour Plate 31). He was one of the most productive and long-lived of all Victorian artists, dying in 1923. His work went through several phases, beginning with a Pre-Raphaelite phase in the 1850s, but then moving towards a more naturalistic style. His later work becomes steadily more impressionistic. He was admired, above all, for his honest and literal renderings of the English countryside and its rivers, especially the Severn near his native town of Worcester. He was also brave enough to paint one of the wettest pictures in English art, 'February Fill-Dyke'. Artists who followed the naturalistic style of Leader were so numerous that only a few of the best can be mentioned. Frederick William Hulme painted very attractive landscapes, often of woodlands. Robert Gallon, John Clayton Adams, and Henry H. Parker were all painters in the naturalistic mould, and all capable of good things. Another above

Colour Plate 31. **BENJAMIN WILLIAMS LEADER.** An Old Manor House by a Stream

average painter was Edward Wilkins Waite, whose landscapes combine a certain rugged honesty with pretty figures of girls. The list of painters of this type is literally endless.

Some landscape painters are difficult to fit into any category, such as John Linnell, who was a friend and pupil of William Blake, and father-in-law of Samuel Palmer. Linnell was a survivor of the Romantic Movement, and also intensely religious, and his landscapes are imbued with a mystical sense of the grandeur of nature. In all his pictures, the figures blend deliberately into the landscape. They have no individuality, no personality, they are simply dwarfed by the forces of nature. Linnell settled in Surrey in 1820, and tried at first to paint biblical scenes set in English landscapes, but the dealers complained that these did not sell. Linnell was forced to turn to pastoral scenes, but tried to imbue them nonetheless with an intensely religious feeling, showing men and animals at work in a timeless and unchanging environment. It proved a highly popular recipe, and when Linnell died in 1882, he was widely regarded as the greatest English landscape painter since Turner. It was also a source of embarrassment to the Royal Academy that Linnell always stubbornly refused to join. His pictures are distinctive for their browny-yellow colours, impressionist technique, and fleecy masses of clouds. One of his favourite subjects was 'A Coming Storm', in which the black, threatening clouds became almost apocalyptic, dwarfing the puny humans who scurry like ants below.

Colour Plate 32. **GEORGE VICAT COLE.** The Hop Gardens

Probably the most popular of all landscape painters from the 1860s onwards was Birket Foster. He was of course a watercolourist, and therefore not strictly relevant to this survey. It is impossible not to mention him, however, because of the extent of his influence. Foster's enchanting visions of the English countryside, with their picturesque cottages, happy villagers and cheerful children, have proved some of the most enduringly popular of all images of England. Their appeal has remained constant throughout the twentieth century, even through the darkest days of modernism. Foster adopted the Pre-Raphaelite method of working over a white ground, using a stipple technique with very fine brushes, and many other watercolourists were to imitate this technique. Foster's followers are too numerous to mention individually, but Joseph Kirkpatrick and Helen Allingham, famous for her watercolours of old cottages, stand out above the rest. Foster's influence on landscape painters remained pervasive for the rest of the century, producing a seemingly limitless vogue for pretty, summery pictures of girls in white dresses and bonnets playing in flower-filled meadows. In the hands of artists of the calibre of B.W. Foster or E.W. Waite, the results could be beautiful; in the hands of lesser men, the results were more likely to be sickly.

A more serious follower of Birket Foster was the influential but short-lived Frederick Walker, who died in 1875 aged only thirty-five. Walker tried to inject more serious and symbolic figures into the pastoral settings of Foster and Allingham. His approach was less sentimental, and he attempted subjects involving distress, poverty and old age — a path down which the prudent Birket Foster would never have followed. Through his work for *The Graphic* magazine, founded in 1869, Walker influenced a whole generation of painters and watercolourists, including the young Van Gogh. Among Walker's closest friends and followers were John William North and Robert Walter MacBeth, both of whom followed the idyllic and pastoral style, but deliberately avoided the prettiness of Birket Foster. The landscape style of all these artists, and of George Heming Mason and the so-called Etruscans who worked in Italy, is the landscape of the Aesthetic Movement — refined, poetic, intelligent, cultured, and with a tinge of underlying concern about social issues.

Many remarkable landscape painters were also to be found in the provinces. Thomas Baker of Leamington, and George Turner of Derbyshire were both well known for painting in their own areas, as were George Marks in Sussex, Thomas Mackay in Cheshire, and William Fraser Garden around St. Ives, Huntingdon. Some artists, like Edmund John Niemann, made a speciality of painting in a particular area, in his case Yorkshire. The scenery of North Wales attracted large numbers of artists, including B.W. Leader and S.R. Percy. The vogue for Scottish landscapes was exploited by the industrious Alfred de Breanski. Scotland produced many fine landscape painters of its own, such as Horatio MacCulloch, Joseph Farquharson, William MacTaggart and Sir David Murray.

Most of the landscape painters I have mentioned so far are essentially English figures. From the 1860s onwards, artists began to travel more, and study on the Continent, and foreign influences began to increase. The Grosvenor Gallery provided a focal point for avant-garde painters, both English and European. In 1886 came the New English Art Club, dedicated to promoting French impressionism. Among its early supporters were Sickert, Wilson Steer, George Clausen, and H.H. La Thangue. In 1899 Stanhope Forbes and his wife Elizabeth founded the Newlyn School in Cornwall, already a flourishing artistic colony devoted to painting fisherfolk in the *plein-air* style of Millet and Bastien-Lepage. Among the early settlers in Newlyn were Frank Bramley, Walter Langley and Henry Scott Tuke. The Barbizon school had its admirers too, such as Alfred East, John Arnesby Brown and William Mark Fisher. The Hague School in Holland was also influential, especially in Scotland among the Glasgow School. By 1900 Robert Bevan was painting Exmoor in the bold Fauvist colours of Gauguin. Victorian landscape really runs across the whole gamut of nineteenth century artistic movements.

Country Life

The painters of country life, village life, and cottage life were almost as numerous as the landscape painters. Some artists painted both types of subject, but in general, the painters of country life form a distinct and separate group of their own. As with landscape paintings, the patrons who bought pictures of country life were mostly town dwellers, who in the main preferred an idealised view of the subject, rather than the reality. The fact that the countryside was certainly not a rural paradise for most of the people who lived and worked in it did not seem to make any difference. The feeling that "Man made the Town, God made the Country" prevailed in art and literature, and still does. The English have always preferred their rusticity idyllic. Those few brave artists who dared to paint the grimmer side of country life were never very popular, either with the critics or the public.

Not all the critics and writers were happy about this situation. "Who is not weary of simpering rusticity?" wrote an *Art Journal* critic in 1856, but his complaints made little difference to the tastes of their patrons or artists. Ragged, barefoot, but resolutely cheerful children continued to grin out from countless canvases; suspiciously pretty girls went on haymaking, filling up pitchers of water, or flirting over stiles. One might be forgiven for thinking that all Victorian farm workers were married to artists' models. Some artists, such as Yeend King, James John Hill, or Charles Sillem Lidderdale, spent whole careers painting pretty farm girls. Resolutely cheerful children were the speciality of William Collins, whose pictures were highly popular in the early Victorian period. William Frederick Witherington was also a popular painter of country life in the 1840s. His pictures are certainly idyllic, but less overtly sentimental than those of Collins; they are always of consistently high quality.

The farm, and farm work, were not in general subjects treated by Victorian painters with any degree of honesty. A Victorian farmyard must have been a messy, muddy and smelly place, but you would not think so looking at the pictures of John Frederick Herring Junior, or Thomas Baker of Leamington. For artists like these, the farmyard was always presented as picturesque and cheerful and the immense popularity of their pictures confirms that this was the kind of farmyard picture the successful merchant wanted to have hanging in his villa. Similar, though not quite so idealised, are the pictures of Thomas Sidney Cooper, who spent his entire life painting cows and sheep (Colour Plate 33). Cooper was one of the best-known and longest-lived of all Victorian painters, and from 1833 to 1902, he exhibited 266 pictures at the Royal Academy, never missing a year. This is still a record, and one never likely to be surpassed. Cooper's pictures can be repetitive, but at their best they have a monumentality and technical finish far superior to most of his rivals. Cooper did for the cow what Landseer had done for the stag. He even painted a large picture entitled 'The Monarch of the Meadows', showing a bull surrounded by docile, recumbent heifers.

The harvest was the high point of the farming year, and for many painters it was therefore an irresistibly picturesque and symbolic subject. Birket Foster's pictures of haymaking and harvesting give the impression that farm work was a perpetual holiday. Other painters invested the harvest with more solemnity and significance. Both George Cole, and his son George Vicat Cole were fond of harvesting scenes, most of which are lyrical celebrations of the English countryside in midsummer (Colour Plate 32). Pictures such as 'Hullo, Largess: 'A Harvest Scene in Norfolk', by William Maw Egley record ancient local customs connected with the harvest that were already disappearing in the nineteenth century. William Edward Millner, a Lincolnshire artist, was one of the few Victorian artists to paint farm work realistically and honestly, including harvest scenes. One of the greatest painters of harvest scenes was John Linnell. For Linnell the harvest, with its symbolic and biblical connotations, was not merely an agricultural event, it was a symbol of God's goodness, as manifested in the bounty of nature, and the fruits of the earth. His harvest scenes are among the most intensely idyllic, and symbolic of all his works (Colour Plate 34).

Almost the only Victorian painter to devote himself wholeheartedly to the theme of the farm worker was George Clausen. His pictures of men in the fields, harvesters, ploughmen, shepherds and bird-scarers, are among the most memorable

Colour Plate 35. **SAMUEL LUKE FILDES.** The Village Wedding

of all images of country life in English art. Clausen studied in Holland, Belgium and Paris, and was impressed with the peasant pictures of Millet and Bastien-Lepage. On his return to England, he painted some of his finest pictures of farm workers, in which the figures have a heroic monumentality quite unequalled in English art. 'Winter Work', now in the Tate Gallery, shows turnip cutters at work in a wet and muddy field. Perhaps more than any picture of the nineteenth century, this painting conveys how it really felt to work in the fields in an English winter. Later Clausen developed a more colourful, impressionistic style, particularly in his pictures of mowers and harvesting (Colour Plate 1). The figures are still monumental, but combined with a flickering brushwork that gives a wonderful impression of sunlight and movement.

Clausen's friend H.H. La Thangue also studied in France, and his agricultural scenes have a similar monumentality, and sense of sympathy for the poor (Colour Plate 36). The youthful Alfred Munnings was also an outstanding painter of country life at the

Colour Plate 33. **THOMAS SIDNEY COOPER.** Canterbury Meadows

Colour Plate 34. **JOHN LINNELL.** Wheat

turn of the century, particularly of horse fairs and gypsies in his native Suffolk.

Two artists brave enough to depict the gloomy side of country life were Hubert von Herkomer and Frank Holl. We have already mentioned Herkomer's famous picture of 1885, 'Hard Times' (Colour Plate 25); it is one of the most powerful of all English social realist pictures. The agricultural depression brought great hardship, and Herkomer wrote that "hundreds of honest workers wandered through the country in search of work . . ." It was one such group that gave Herkomer the idea for his picture.

Village life in all its aspects was a popular subject with many artists. Most of them were quite happy to perpetuate the idealised view of the village as a happy, picturesque and bustling place. Birket Foster and Helen Allingham, of course, projected this view, but another interesting group of artists who specialised in village life was the so-called Cranbrook Colony. This was a group of artists who settled in Cranbrook in Kent, and devoted themselves to scenes of domestic and village life. The leader of the group was Thomas Webster, a prolific painter of cottage scenes and other everyday scenes of village life. Frederick Daniel Hardy, was another member of this group, and technically the best artist among them. His early interiors have an extraordinary clarity and precision of observation comparable only to the Dutch masters of the seventeenth century. Other members of the colony included George Bernard O'Neill, George Smith and John Callcott Horsley, painter of 'Showing a Preference', a Victorian classic of flirtation in the countryside. Other painters of village life are too numerous to mention, but one artistic family is worthy of record — the Hayllars. James Hayllar and his four talented daughters, Jessica, Edith, Mary and Kate, lived on the Thames at Wallingford in Oxfordshire. They all painted well and, as we have seen, took for their subjects both their own domestic life, and the life of the villagers of Wallingford. Fortunately for us, they also photographed all their works and preserved them in albums, which survive. Their pictures form one of the most remarkable and delightful records of middle-class life in a Victorian country town.

Not far away, in the village of Aston Tirrold, Luke Fildes painted one of the grandest and most joyous of all Victorian country pictures 'The Village Wedding' (Colour Plate 35) to show that he could paint happy subjects, as well as gloomy social realist ones. 'The Village Wedding' was painted in 1883, but Fildes has deliberately set the picture about fifty years earlier, in an imaginary golden age. This technique was exactly that used by Victorian novelists, such as George Eliot, who set their novels in some supposedly happier, more idyllic period around the beginning of the nineteenth century.

The cottage was for the Victorians a cherished symbol of the innocence they felt they had lost, the epitome of a way of life they knew to be disappearing. It was one of their most sacred myths, an icon at the heart of their concept of country life. Paintings extolling the joys of cottage life were the most common of all Victorian narrative pictures. Again, the painters of such subjects are so numerous that only a few of the better ones can be mentioned. Helen Allingham and Birket Foster, as already mentioned, were the best-known delineators of the picturesque old cottage. They had many imitators, but few equals. Among the best of the 'cottage door' painters were Arthur Claude Strachan, Henry J. Johnston, Ethel Hughes, William

Plate 9. **GEORGE ELGAR HICKS.** Asleep in the Cornfield

Affleck and Charles Edward Wilson. The Cranbrook painters, as we have already seen, painted many cottage interiors, especially F.D. Hardy and George Smith. Among the other innumerable practitioners of this genre were Joseph Clark, Charles James Lewis, William Henry Knight, William Henry Midwood, Carlton Alfred Smith and Henry Tozer. Their pictures are invariably happy and cheerful, with cottagers engaged in domestic chores, or some cottage industry, such as spinning. This was, of course, largely make-believe, as most of the cottage crafts were dead by the late Victorian period. Another essential element was rustic piety. The Victorians clung to the idea that the rustic was a simple, pious soul, who went to church every Sunday and read the family bible every day. Hence many cottage pictures show the family gathered round to hear grandfather read from the Good Book.

The Victorian obsession with the cottage is inseparable from the idea of childhood. In the Victorian scheme of things, a cottage was the best place to be born. It might be simple, and uncomfortable, but it was a happy and innocent atmosphere, and the

Colour Plate 36. **HENRY HERBERT LA THANGUE.** A Sussex Orchard

Colour Plate 37. **WILLIAM H. SNAPE.** Cottage Interior

Victorians valued purity and innocence above all else. In almost all pictures of cottage and village life, children play a major part. The nineteenth century produced many of the most delightful pictures of children in the whole of English art, and many of them are pictures of country children (Plate 9 and Colour Plate 37). Once again, only a few of the better artists can be mentioned. Sophie Anderson made her name with her delightful pictures of children at play in the countryside. John Morgan and his son Fred Morgan were both prolific painters of children and their games, as were William Bromley, William Hemsley, Harry Brooker, George Washington Brownlow, and many others. Very few of these pictures even hint at the fact that most of these children would be sent out to work in the fields by the age of eight or nine. Frederic J. Shields's painting 'One of Our Breadwatchers' acts as a stern and necessary reminder. At Porlock, in Somerset, Shields had observed the practice of leaving children out in the snow all day to scare birds off the newly-sown corn. His picture shows one of these poor children, sitting in a rudely constructed shelter of gorse and hurdles, trying to keep warm by a tiny fire. The Education Acts of the 1870s and 1880s gradually put an end to these abuses, as parents were forced by law to send their children to school until they were older. The village school, or dame school, also provided many Victorian painters with a fertile theme.

Plate 10. **GEORGE SAMUEL ELGOOD.** The Gardens at Melbourne Hall, Derbyshire

Still-life, Flowers and Gardens

Many Victorian artists tried their hand occasionally at still-life or flower painting, but as with so many areas in Victorian painting, there were specialists who devoted whole careers to this branch of art. Many of the best still-life artists were watercolourists, and therefore fall outside the range of this survey. Mention has to be made, however, of William Henry Hunt, or Bird's-Nest Hunt, as he has become known. He was the inventor of the small, detailed still-life, minutely observed and painted with a stipple technique, which usually included a bird's nest, flowers, blossom or fruit, set against a mossy background. It was a recipe to be repeated endlessly by Victorian artists for the rest of the century, and sums up perfectly the Victorian combination of reverence for nature and desire for scientific exactitude. Hunt himself embodied the serious Victorian approach to still-life painting, declaring that he felt "really frightened" when about to paint a flower. Hunt had numerous pupils and followers, notably John Sherrin, William Hough, and the three Clares, George, Oliver and Vincent, who mainly painted in oil. William Cruickshank's small and minute watercolours, often painted on ivory, owe much to Hunt's example. Many Victorian lady artists painted flowers and still-life, notably Helen Cordelia Coleman, and Mary Ann Duffield, wife of the still-life painter William Duffield. There was also a distinct school of Victorian artists who specialised in gardens. Here again, they were mainly watercolourists. The chief exponents of garden painting were George Samuel Elgood (Plate 10), Ernest Arthur Rowe, Beatrice Parsons, Thomas Hunn, and various members of the Bedfordshire Stannard family, notably Lilian and Theresa Sylvester.

Plate 11
GEORGE LANCE.
Still-life

Confusingly, there was another family of painters called Stannard, in East Anglia, though the two were not connected. Several of the female Stannards were flower painters. Mrs Joseph Stannard (Emily Coppin) and her daughter Emily worked in the traditional Dutch style of Van Huysum. Eloise Harriet Stannard, the daughter of the landscape painter Alfred Stannard, painted both flowers and fruit with great accuracy and a luscious sense of colour. East Anglia also produced one of the most popular of all Victorian still-life painters, Edward Ladell, who lived in Colchester. He and his wife Ellen developed a highly successful recipe for still-life on the Dutch pattern, using the same props again and again — fruit, a casket, a glass, nuts or other objects on a marble ledge draped with a rug, beautifully observed, and with a richness of colour that was totally Victorian.

The two greatest exponents of still-life in the Victorian period were George Lance and his pupil, William Duffield. Lance began his career as a pupil of Benjamin Robert Haydon, and aspired to grand historical subjects. He soon found that his still-life pictures of fruit were more saleable, and so devoted the rest of his career to producing them (Plate 11). His pupil William Duffield studied in Antwerp, and from the Flemish painters Snyders and de Vos he developed a Victorian version of the grand still-life, incorporating fruit, flowers, vegetables, dead game, and sometimes figures in historical costume. Duffield died young in 1863, reputedly from the evil smell of a dead stag which he was painting in his studio.

Duffield lived and worked in Bath, and the provinces produced many other artists specialising in fruit and flowers. William J. Muckley was from Manchester, as were the two Mutrie sisters, all of whom painted colourful and showy flower pictures. Another talented flower painter was John Wainwright, but virtually nothing is known about him. Albert Durer Lucas, the son of a Victorian sculptor, lived in the New Forest in Hampshire, and was one of the very few Victorian artists to take a serious interest in wild flowers, especially heathers.

Colour Plate 38. **GEORGE EARL.** King's Cross — Going North

Sporting and Animal Painting

As with everything else, the Victorian period was a golden age for sporting and animal painting. Not only hunting, racing, shooting and fishing had their specialist schools of painters, but almost every other sport was depicted on canvas — tennis, croquet, archery, even golf. Every kind of animal, both wild and domestic, was painted by Victorian artists, and many artists made a living painting dogs and cats. The early nineteenth century was also the golden age of the stagecoach, and the great coaching painter James Pollard lived until 1867, well into the railway age. The tradition of coaching paintings was carried on right through the century by Charles Cooper Henderson, George Wright and J.C. Maggs.

The foundations of English sporting art were laid in the eighteenth century by John Wootton, George Stubbs, the Sartorius family and others. The tradition was carried on through Ben Marshall, Sawrey Gilpin, Philip Reinagle, Dean Wolstenholme, Henry Alken and James Ward, most of whom lived into the Victorian period. The most successful Victorian hunting and racing painter was John Ferneley, who lived most of his life in Melton Mowbray, Leicestershire, headquarters of the great hunting packs of the Midlands. Although he exhibited in London, Ferneley was supported entirely by private patrons, painting horse portraits, hunting scenes and racing subjects. The same might be said of many other sporting painters, such as the Alken family, R.B. Davis, Harry Hall, Thomas Bretland, F.C. Turner, John and David Dalby of York, and the two Barrauds, William and Henry. Sir Francis Grant has already been mentioned as a fashionable portrait painter, but he first made his name with sporting pictures, in particular 'The Melton Hunt Breakfast' of 1834, and 'H.M. Staghounds on Ascot Heath', painted in 1837. He was also a highly accomplished and elegant painter of equestrian portraits.

After Ferneley, the most prolific sporting and animal painter of the Victorian age

Colour Plate 39. **EDWIN HENRY LANDSEER.** Scene in Braemar — Highland Deer

was John Frederick Herring, Senior. He studied with another animal painter, Abraham Cooper, and became a popular painter of racehorses, painting the winners of the Derby and the St. Leger for many years. He also painted stable yard scenes, and farmyard scenes, which were closely imitated by his son J.F. Herring, Junior. Herring Senior also made many charming small studies of goats, rabbits, ducks, birds and other animals.

Members of the royal family were regular patrons of sporting and animal painters, and employed J.F. Herring, as well as Robert Morley and R.B. Davis to paint their horses. Thomas Sidney Cooper was called in to paint the royal herd at Osborne, and F.W. Keyl some of the other animals. Later the Queen's favourite dog painter was

Charles Burton Barber.

The greatest royal favourite was, of course, Edwin Landseer, who has left us with many delightful pictures of the royal family and its pets, at Windsor, Osborne, and Balmoral. Landseer was a child prodigy, and entered the RA schools at the age of fourteen. From the first, he was keen to paint animals, and in 1824 C.R. Leslie took him to Scotland and introduced him to Sir Walter Scott. The highlands made a great impression on the young painter, and Scottish subjects, especially stags, were to become his signature tune (Colour Plate 39). Enormous numbers of engravings were made of his Scottish pictures, such as 'Monarch of the Glen' or 'The Stag at Bay', making them some of the most familiar images in Victorian art. Landseer also painted sentimental pictures of dogs such as 'Dignity and Impudence'. His animal pictures contain a mixture of cruelty and sentimentality that is typically Victorian, and which makes him a difficult artist for the twentieth century to understand. Eventually, Landseer went mad, overwhelmed by drink and unfinished commissions, leaving a huge fortune of £200,000.

Many artists tried to imitate Landseer, few succeeded. One who did was the Liverpool artist, Richard Ansdell. His highland scenes are not as dramatic, or as bloodthirsty, as Landseer's and he tended to concentrate on the more peaceful aspects of highland life, such as gamekeepers or sheep drovers. Another Liverpool animal painter was William Huggins, who pronounced that "if I had Landseer through my hands for six months I could have made a man of him!" Huggins's own pictures, generally of lions or hens, rather belie such boastfulness. William Strutt, who spent some time painting the out-back in Australia, was also a noted painter of wild animals. Landseer's successors were Briton Riviere and J.C. Dollman. Riviere was an ambitious artist who succeeded in combining animals with historical and mythological subjects. Charles Jones, known as Sheep Jones, spent a lifetime painting sheep; Henry Stacy Marks preferred exotic birds. One of the most subtle observers of animals, especially birds, was the Glasgow artist Joseph Crawhall. His rapid studies, drawn in watercolour on linen or silk, are marvels of observation and brevity.

Among country society, there was a steady demand for pictures of the gentry engaged in sporting pursuits. Artists such as Heywood Hardy and John Charlton catered for this market. There was also a huge market for pictures of dogs and foxhounds. Thomas Blinks, John Emms and J.S. Noble all specialised in hounds; terriers were the province of Arthur Wardle and George Armfield. The Earl family all painted dogs; George Earl, as we now know, was capable of better things, and painted the two outstanding railway pictures, 'King's Cross — Going North' (Colour Plate 38) and 'Perth Station — Coming South', now in the Railway Museum in York. His daughter, Maud Earl, specialised in toy dogs and unusual breeds. Cats, too, were not neglected, and both Frank Paton and Horatio Couldery devoted most of their careers to painting cats and especially kittens.

Marine and Coastal Painting

Ships and the sea have always been important to England, and never more so than in the nineteenth century. During Victoria's reign England's position as a great naval and mercantile power reached its apogee, and it was an equally rich period for naval and marine painters. The great ports of London, Bristol and Liverpool were among the biggest and busiest in the world, places of excitement and romance, and an obvious attraction to painters like Atkinson Grimshaw, famous for his moonlit views of Liverpool Docks.

Marine painters of the eighteenth century were mainly concerned with the precise delineation of naval battles and ships. This tradition continued into the nineteenth century, but parallel with it grew an increasing fascination with the sea itself, with storms, picturesque coasts, sailing boats and the lives of fishermen. The sea was a great source of inspiration to Turner, who lived fifteen years into the Victorian period. No Victorian artist could match the romantic epics of Turner, but he had numerous followers and admirers, such as Sir Augustus Wall Callcott and Clarkson Stanfield. Both painted large river and coastal scenes which owe an obvious debt to Turner. Stanfield served in the navy, and then became a painter of theatrical scenery. A close friend of Dickens, he designed much of the scenery for Dickens's private theatricals. Stanfield painted both shipping and coastal scenes, as well as naval battles. His huge picture 'The Battle of Trafalgar' of 1863 hangs in the old United Services Club in Pall Mall. Stanfield died soon after his great friend David Roberts, and his pupil was Edward William Cooke, a prolific painter of coastal scenes (Colour Plate 40) and Venetian views. Cooke was technically a finer painter than Stanfield, and employed a more daring range of colours, particularly when painting sunsets.

Like Stanfield, George Chambers was a northerner, born in Whitby, who also served in the navy as a young man. On coming south, he also worked for a while as a theatrical scenery painter. His pictures of ships and naval actions were very popular with naval officers, who appreciated his expert knowledge of ships and the sea (Colour Plate 41).

A naval officer who also painted was Captain Richard Beechey, a son of Sir William Beechey. He eventually rose to the rank of admiral, but combined this with a career as a painter, exhibiting at the Royal Academy from 1832 to 1877. He seemed to like painting pictures of rough weather, shipwrecks and storms. Among other mid-Victorian marine painters, William Adolphus Knell deserves a mention. He was a prolific painter of river and coastal scenes, both in England and Europe. For Queen Victoria he painted 'The Landing of Prince Albert at Dover' and 'The Review of the Fleet at Spithead'. Also prolific was Edwin Hayes, born in Bristol, but later a member of the RHA in Dublin. He exhibited at the Royal Academy from 1855 to 1904, specialising in coastal scenes with fishing boats.

The tradition of painting warships and naval battles was continued by John Christian Schetky. He taught at both Sandhurst and the Royal Naval College at Portsmouth, and was a favourite with William IV, the Sailor King. In 1844 he was appointed Marine Painter in Ordinary to Queen Victoria. He exhibited ship pictures and naval incidents, old and new, at the Royal Academy for over sixty years. Another painter of a similar type was R.B. Spencer.

Straightforward ship portraits were much in demand, and almost every port had its local painter. Liverpool produced a number of good ship painters, such as Samuel Walters, Joseph Heard, and W.H. Yorke. It was the Mersey that was also to inspire many of Atkinson Grimshaw's finest night scenes. Joseph Walter was the leading

Colour Plate 40. **EDWARD WILLIAM COOKE.** Dutch Trawlers at Anchor, Scheveningen

Bristol painter, and W.J. Huggins was well-known in London for his pictures of ships on the Thames. Hull produced a number of good marine painters, such as Henry Redmore and John Ward of Hull. Most of these artists painted sailing ships, but William Clark of Glasgow made a speciality of steamships and other modern vessels built in the Glasgow shipyards. Another provincial artist, of a rather higher calibre, was John Wilson Carmichael of Newcastle. Carmichael settled in London, and travelled in Holland, Italy and the Baltic. He also covered the Crimean War for *The Illustrated London News*. In his early career he painted naval battles, but later expanded his repertoire to include all kinds of coastal views, shipping scenes, and landscapes. He particularly liked painting the north-east coast, and the east coast of Scotland. He used a much brighter range of colours than the traditional naval painters, who tended to stick to the dark tones of Van der Velde and Monamy.

The Pre-Raphaelites did not make much of an impact on marine painting, although John Brett in his later years devoted himself entirely to coastal scenes, in which the rocks are rendered with true Ruskinian exactitude. He also painted a number of very large sea-pieces, which can at their best be impressively panoramic. One of the very few artists to devote himself to the pure sea-piece was Henry Moore, the brother of Albert Joseph Moore. David James made a speciality of painting waves. Pre-Raphaelite influence is more discernible in paintings of rocks and cliffs, while William Dyce's 'Pegwell Bay' (Colour Plate 10) is the most photographic of all Pre-Raphaelite landscapes.

Other coastal painters are so numerous that only a few of them can be mentioned. James Clarke Hook was a painter much esteemed in his day; James Webb was also

Colour Plate 41. **GEORGE CHAMBERS, Jnr.** The Thames at Greenwich

popular and successful. His studio sales at Christie's after his death lasted for three days. Charles Napier Hemy was born in Newcastle, but settled in Cornwall, and his strong, vigorous style has affinities with the Newlyn School. His style was continued by his more famous pupil, Montague Dawson. Many of the Newlyn painters painted coastal and harbour scenes, and will be mentioned later.

The life of the fisherman seemed to the Victorians full of heroism and danger, and the picture of wives waiting for the return of the boats became a well-worn cliché. Frank Holl and Frank Bramley were among the more distinguished exponents, but numerous others tried it, including Thomas Brooks, Thomas Rose Miles and Robert Jobling. Robert Weir Allan and John R. Reid were among the many Scottish painters who found fisherfolk a profitable vein. The Scots also produced their own distinctive brand of coastal painters, of whom the most distinguished were Peter Graham and Sir William MacTaggart.

Marine painting continued to be a popular branch of art up to the end of the century, and is still thriving today. After the death of Schetky in 1874, Sir Oswald Brierley was appointed Marine Painter to the Queen. As well as recording royal visits and royal yachts, he painted historical naval battles with a strongly patriotic flavour. William Lionel Wyllie was one of the best marine painters of the late nineteenth century, and lived on until 1931. He is particularly known for his busy port scenes of the Thames and the Port of London. His picture of 'Toil, Glitter, Grime and Wealth on a Flowing Tide', now in the Tate Gallery, gives a wonderful impression of the busy life on the Thames, when London was the biggest port in the world.

Plate 12. **ERNEST CROFTS.** From Quatre Bras to Waterloo

Military and Battle Painting

The Victorians were only involved in one major war, the Crimean campaign, but hardly a year of Victoria's reign went by without a colonial campaign in some part of the empire. All this is reflected in a flourishing school of military and battle painters, never a coherent group, but nonetheless worthy of mention. Specific regimental uniforms, groups, and battles were recorded by specialists such as Orlando Norie and Richard Simkin.

The Napoleonic wars still loomed large in the Victorian consciousness. From David Wilkie's 'Chelsea Pensioners Reading the Waterloo Dispatch' onwards, Victorian artists never seemed to tire of painting the Napoleonic campaigns, and especially the Battle of Waterloo (Colour Plate 42). George Jones and Thomas Jones Barker were both military painters specialising in these subjects. Daniel Maclise's great murals in the Houses of Parliament of 'The Meeting of Wellington and Blucher' and 'The Death of Nelson' enshrined these two events for ever in the nation's pantheon. The obsession with Napoleon seemed to increase as the century wore on, and even later Victorian painters such as Ernest Crofts (Plate 12), Robert Alexander Hillingford and Richard Caton Woodville found a ready audience for Napoleonic battles. Robert Gibb, the Scottish painter who painted the original 'The Thin Red Line', also painted 'The Retreat from Moscow', a subject which seemed to have a particular appeal to the Victorians. All of these artists also looked further back in English history, to the Civil War, the Armada, or the Wars of the Spanish Succession, in search of subjects. Andrew Carrick Gow was one of many artists to paint the battles of the Civil War, and scenes of the life of Cromwell, who was seen by the Victorians as a champion of English democracy.

The Crimea was too far away for most artists, except for the illustrators sent out by the magazines. Jerry Barrett managed to capture the prevailing mood of patriotism with his two pictures 'The Mission of Mercy — Florence Nightingale Receiving the Wounded at Scutari in 1856' and 'Queen Victoria Visiting the Military Hospital at Chatham', where she met some of the Crimean wounded. Both pictures were

Colour Plate 42. **HENRY NELSON O'NEIL.** Before Waterloo

enormously popular through engravings. The Crimea was to inspire the most famous of all Victorian battle painters, Elizabeth Thompson, later Lady Butler. Her picture of 'The Roll Call', showing guardsmen in the Crimean winter, was the sensation of the Royal Academy of 1874, and made the artist famous overnight. Lady Butler devoted the rest of her career to military subjects, both Crimean and Napoleonic. 'Scotland for Ever', showing the Scots Greys charging at Waterloo, has become perhaps the most famous image of that battle. Lady Butler looked further afield, both to Egypt and to India, and her most ambitious work, 'The Remnants of an Army', shows the sole survivor of the terrible retreat from Kabul in the first Afghan war.

The Indian Mutiny also deeply stirred the Victorian imagination, although very few artists were actually there. Nonetheless, several memorable images of the Mutiny were created, in particular Henry Nelson O'Neil's 'Eastward Ho! August 1857' and 'Home Again', both already mentioned. The heroism of the English women in India was commemorated by Joseph Noel Paton in his picture 'In Memoriam', a picture which was lost for many years, but now happily rediscovered. 'The Relief of Lucknow' was duly recorded by Thomas Jones Barker, and other incidents recreated by Frederick Goodall and Abraham Solomon, not very convincingly, but authentically enough to interest a Victorian audience.

Closer to home was the Volunteer Movement, which began in the 1860s in response to the imperialist ambitions of Napoleon III. Volunteer Parades provided numerous Victorian painters with an opportunity to depict men in uniform, notably 'Volunteers at Firing Point' by Henry Tanworth Wells, and 'Volunteers' by Arthur Boyd Houghton.

Many of the later colonial wars, in Egypt, the Sudan, and Africa were recorded by such artists as William Barnes Wollen, Caton Woodville and Robert Talbot Kelly. Their pictures are usually jingoistic in tone, and show natives in full flight from the might of British arms. The British have always mythologised their defeats even more than their victories, and the unfortunate 'Battle of Isandhlwana' was recorded by Charles Edwin Fripp, and 'The Defence of Rorkes Drift' by Caton Woodville. Many of these artists went on to paint the lamentable engagements of the Boer War, which dented for ever the Victorian legend of military invincibility.

Travellers and Topographers
The Victorians were inveterate travellers. There was hardly a corner of the world they did not penetrate, and the English were also in the forefront of exploration, both of Africa and the polar regions. For the middle classes, travel became available to everyone as never before in history, thanks to the steamer, the railway, and Cook's tours. In painting, this resulted in an insatiable demand for pictures of foreign places, and even more for pictures of their exotic, colourful inhabitants. Some artists became specialists in particular countries — John Phillip in Spain, William Callow in France, David Roberts and J.F. Lewis in the Middle East. A painter like Edward Lear became virtually a perpetual traveller and topographer.

Europe still offered great opportunities to painters, particularly its cities, old buildings and cathedrals. Ruskin, above all, had taught the Victorians to look at medieval architecture, particularly the cathedrals of northern France. Bonington was long dead, but his inspiration lived on in the works of Thomas Shotter Boys and William Callow. William Wyld lived in Paris, and specialised in Parisian views. The

Rhine was another hugely popular area, painted by artists such as James Duffield Harding, James Webb, and George Clarkson Stanfield. For most educated travellers, France and Germany were only preludes to the ultimate goal of the Grand Tour — Italy, and above all, Venice. Innumerable Victorian artists spent time in Italy, Samuel Palmer and John Scarlett Davis to name but two. Frederic Leighton and his friends 'The Etruscans' spent considerable periods in Rome painting the surrounding campagna. Venice provided some painters like James Holland, Edward Pritchett and Henry Woods with subjects for a lifetime.

In the nineteenth century Spain was still an unknown and unexplored country, and one which fascinated the Victorians. The stock Victorian recipe for a Spanish picture was of a grinning girl wearing a lace mantilla and with a rose behind her ear. Artists such as J.B. Burgess and Robert Kemm made a profession of painting these modern "mayas". The Scottish painter, John Phillip, made a much more serious attempt to depict Spanish life, though his pictures too can strike the modern viewer as stage sets for an indifferent production of *Carmen*. He was in fact a highly talented and natural artist, and some of his Spanish works are superbly painted. Not for nothing did he earn the sobriquet of Spanish Phillip. The Victorian vogue for Spanish subjects has never revived, and seems unlikely ever to do so.

The Victorians were even more fascinated by the Middle East, and this was an area that attracted many of the greatest artists and topographers of the nineteenth century. Victorian motives for liking the Middle East were extremely mixed. For some, like Holman Hunt, the interest was above all religious and biblical; for others, such as J.F. Lewis, it was the exotic flavour of Arab life that was the attraction. The Victorian gentleman in his top hat also enjoyed the frisson of examining pictures extolling the delights of the harem, or the attractions of slave girls and dancers, and there were plenty of artists ready to cater for this vogue too. Two of the earliest painters to travel in the Middle East were Scotsmen — David Wilkie and David Roberts. Wilkie visited Turkey and Egypt, and died on board ship on his way home in 1841, an event commemorated by Turner in one of his most dramatic pictures, 'Peace — Burial at Sea'. Wilkie managed only to complete a few sketches, including two brilliant portraits of the Sultan of Turkey, and the Pasha of Egypt, Mohamet Ali.

David Roberts was already much travelled by the time he first arrived in the Middle East in 1838. He had already made a name for himself as a topographer in France, Spain and North Africa. He spent a year in Egypt and the Holy Land, industriously making sketches wherever he went, which were to last him a lifetime. The first fruits of his labours were the set of six volumes of *Views in the Holy Land, Syria, Idumea, Arabia, Egypt and Nubia* published between 1842 and 1849. Roberts lacked either the brilliance of Lewis or the spontaneity of Wilkie, but he made up for it by his dogged Scots professionalism. His views are done to a formula; the buildings are accurate, the groups of figures tasteful, but one Roberts view can look very much like another, particularly in the colouring (Colour Plate 43). His view of the Middle East was a sanitised, Cook's tour view, tailored to the outlook of the Victorian middle classes.

Infinitely more brilliant are the extraordinary oils and watercolours painted by John Frederick Lewis in Egypt. Like Roberts, Lewis had also made his name painting in Spain. In 1841, he set off for Egypt, by way of Corfu, Albania, Greece and Turkey. He found Cairo so much to his taste that he bought a house, donned

Colour Plate 43. **DAVID ROBERTS.** Philae, Egypt

Arab dress, took to Arab habits, and remained there for the next nine years. It was here that he painted his wonderful studies of Arab life, one of which, 'The Hareem', caused a sensation at the Old Watercolour Society Exhibition of 1850. Although he had never met any of the Pre-Raphaelites, the brilliance of his watercolours and his technique of using pure, bright colours caused his name to be linked with theirs. Lewis returned to England in 1851, and became President of the Watercolour Society in 1855. After this he turned entirely to painting in oils, drawing constantly on his memories of the Middle East for his subjects (Colour Plate 44).

Also in the Middle East in the 1840s was the Bristol artist, William James Müller. His rich palette and love of chiaroscuro are more akin to Turner and Delacroix than to Lewis or Roberts. It was the exotic, romantic side of the Middle East that appealed to him, but many of his pictures were left unfinished, and his sketches incomplete as a result of his untimely death in 1845.

Holman Hunt made his first trip to the Holy Land in 1854. His purpose was simple — to find authentic settings for biblical pictures. But he too was seduced by the exotic life of Jerusalem and Palestine, and became fascinated by Judaic history and ritual. It was this obsession that was to shape all his biblical pictures, from 'The Scapegoat' and 'The Finding of the Saviour in the Temple' to 'The Shadow of the Cross'. The landscape was also to inspire some of his finest watercolours. The element of danger only added spice to the adventure of painting in the Middle East; by the Dead Sea Hunt worked on 'The Scapegoat' with a loaded gun across his knees. Hunt's follower Thomas Seddon has left us with almost the only Pre-Raphaelite landscape of the Middle East, 'Jerusalem and the Valley of Jehoshaphat'. This was painted in 1854, on Seddon's first trip together with Holman Hunt. In 1856, Seddon returned and died of a fever in Cairo, a reminder of just how dangerous foreign travel could be for the intrepid Victorian artist.

Another painter who spent time in Cairo was Frederick Goodall, who exploited the vogue both for Egyptian views, and biblical scenes. Although not an inspired recorder of the Middle East, Goodall's pictures made him both rich and successful

Colour Plate 44. **JOHN FREDERICK LEWIS.** The Midday Meal, Cairo

Colour Plate 45. **EDWARD LEAR.** Corfu

during the 1870s and 1880s. His travelling companion was Carl Haag, a German artist popular with Victoria and Albert, who painted many of their family outings in the highlands at Balmoral. In the Middle East he painted scenes of Arab and Bedouin life, not as brilliantly as Lewis, but with a high degree of accuracy and competence.

The most peripatetic Victorian artist of all was the painter-cum-nonsense poet, Edward Lear. From his first continental trip of 1837 to his death in 1887, Lear was almost constantly travelling, sometimes visiting five or six countries a year. In addition to all the usual European places, Lear specialised in wild and inaccessible regions, such as Corsica, Greece and Albania. He was particularly fond of Corfu (Colour Plate 45) and the Lebanon. In 1873 he travelled to India and Ceylon, where the scenery delighted him, and he was to paint some of his most spectacular landscapes. He took painting lessons from Holman Hunt, and his finished oils can suffer from hard colours and an over-laboured surface, nor was he good at figures. But at their best, some of his views in India and the Middle East are quite unrivalled for their panoramic sweep and grandeur. His more natural medium was watercolour, which he laid over a rapid network of pen-lines and notes. These works are quite unmistakable, and show his artistic handwriting at its most characteristic. Of the many other Victorian artists who travelled in India, none could equal Lear. Mortimer Menpes, a pupil of Whistler, made many delightful studios of Indian customs and costume, though he is now better known for his views in Japan. Val Prinsep also visited India, and recorded the Durbar ceremonies of 1876.

George Chinnery is now chiefly remembered for his pictures of the Far East, but he also spent twenty-three years in Calcutta. Chinnery was a colourful character, who began life as a portrait painter in England and in Dublin, but fled to India to escape both his wife and his debts. In Calcutta he became well-known as a portrait and landscape painter, and also as an observer of Indian life. But eventually his family caught up with him, and he fled east yet again, arriving in Macao in 1825. Here he remained for the rest of his life, occasionally visiting Canton and Hong Kong. Wherever he went, he made innumerable drawings of the Chinese, making notes in a shorthand of his own invention. He painted portraits of Chinese officials and English merchants; he painted views, market scenes and junks, usually in watercolour. He was the most prolific, and most perceptive, observer of Chinese life in the nineteenth century, and his work is now highly admired and prized in the Far East.

Impressionism and the Newlyn School

One of the chief characteristics of Victorian art in the mid-century was its insularity. During the 1860s and 1870s this increasingly began to change, as more and more artists went to study abroad. The chief artistic mecca was Paris, and George Du Maurier's highly popular novel *Trilby* described the joys of bohemian life to be found there. One of the artists in the so-called Trilby Gang was Whistler who, although American-born, was to spend most of his career in London. He was an early convert to French ideas, and was important in bringing these ideas to London. He developed his own highly refined version of French Impressionism, in which Japanese influence played a large part. At the opening of the Grosvenor Gallery in 1877, it was

Whistler's pictures that caused the greatest furore, and led to the celebrated Whistler v. Ruskin trial. For a brief and turbulent period, Whistler was also President of the Society of British Artists. However, he was more important as a leader of the Aesthetic Movement than as an Impressionist.

During the 1870s and 1880s the influence of French art began to grow, culminating in the founding of the New English Art Club in 1886. This was devoted specifically to the propagation of French ideas in general, and French Impressionism in particular. Among its earliest members and exhibitors were Walter Richard Sickert, Philip Wilson Steer, Fred Brown, T.B. Kennington, W.J. Laidlay and George Clausen. From the start, English Impressionism was a diverse and complex movement, and it is difficult to describe it as a coherent school. It was more a loose association of individuals, united in their admiration for French art, but very varied in their responses to it. Much depended on whether you were a follower of Degas, Manet or Monet, or whether you preferred figure subjects to landscape. Many English artists were more attracted to the *plein-air* pictures of peasant life, of which Millet and Bastien-Lepage were the most famous exponents. These more traditionally-minded artists were certainly not prepared to follow Impressionism down the path to Post-Impressionism, as did a number of English and Scottish artists in the late Victorian period. The Scottish Colourists and the Glasgow School were even more enthusiastic converts to Impressionism than many of their English contemporaries.

Artistic colonies became fashionable in France in the mid-century, as places where like-minded younger artists could go and paint together in the summer months. Many English artists visited these colonies in France, and it was not long before similar colonies sprang up in England. Easily the most important was Newlyn, a small fishing village close to Penzance, in Cornwall. Newlyn was first "discovered" in the early 1880s by two Birmingham artists, Walter Langley and Edwin Harris. Through the decade, its popularity grew, and among the earliest to arrive were Stanhope Forbes, Thomas Cooper Gotch, Frank Bramley, Fred Hall, Ralph Todd, Henry Scott Tuke, and Elizabeth Armstrong, later to become the wife of Stanhope Forbes. By 1884 Forbes was already writing that "Newlyn is a sort of English Concarneau . . ." The Newlyn artists were dedicated, like Bastien-Lepage and the French *plein-air* painters, to depicting the life of ordinary country people as honestly and truthfully as possible. The fisherfolk and farmers of Newlyn proved ideal for the purpose, and some of the early Newlyn pictures look as if they might have been painted in Brittany rather than Cornwall. To match their outlook, the Newlyn painters favoured the rugged technique of the square brush, and painted outdoors, so as to capture effects of light and atmosphere as truthfully as possible. Eventually, Newlyn did produce its own distinctive brand of picture — French realism with an English accent. Frank Bramley's 'A Hopeless Dawn' and Forbes's 'The Health of the Bride' (Colour Plate 46) are two examples of Newlyn at its best and most characteristic. Although numerous Newlyn artists exhibited at the New English Art Club, most of the best Newlyn pictures were exhibited at the Academy. This was partly because the Academy was a better place to sell pictures, but also because Forbes and others soon became disenchanted with the NEAC, seeing it as too dominated by Sickert and the other painters of low life. The Newlyn artists

Colour Plate 46. **STANHOPE FORBES.** The Health of the Bride

preferred not only the bracing air of Cornwall, but also its more healthy subject-matter. Newlyn went on to be an important artistic centre in the twentieth century as well, home to such painters as Laura Knight, Harold Harvey, and Lamorna Birch.

Not all late Victorian painters went to Newlyn. Sickert, Steer and the Francophiles preferred Dieppe. Others went to Staithes, on the coast of Yorkshire, or to Cullercoats in Northumberland. The Glasgow Boys had their own Scottish preferences, such as Cockburnspath, or the Hebrides. Some artists simply preferred to be independent, and avoided joining any colony or group. Clausen and La Thangue, two of the greatest English Impressionist painters, followed their own individual paths, and tended to exhibit at the Royal Academy. The same might be said of the two Stotts, William and Edwin, who produced their own very personal versions of Impressionism, without belonging to any distinct group.

As always, in English art it is its diversity that makes it interesting, its tendency to produce individualists, as well as groups. The Newlyn School was only one strand among many in late Victorian art, and has to be seen against the background of Pre-Raphaelitism, classicism, and the Aesthetic Movement. Only then can one appreciate just how dazzlingly varied and complex the story of late Victorian art really is.

Colour Plate 47. **JOHN GILBERT.** The Field of the Cloth of Gold

Victorian Watercolour Paintings

The Watercolour Societies

A history of Victorian art would not be complete without reference to watercolour painting. It was a rich and productive period for watercolours, as it was for oils. Many artists, like Turner, to choose an obvious example, were equally happy in either medium. Some artists such as William Henry Hunt, Birket Foster and Helen Allingham, were watercolour specialists; others such as Albert Goodwin, were predominantly watercolourists, but occasionally painted in oils. The majority painted in both mediums. Most of the Pre-Raphaelites, for example, used watercolour as well as oil. What varied considerably was the use they made of watercolour. Whereas Millais used watercolour mainly to make replicas of his oils, Holman Hunt developed his watercolour landscapes, especially of the Middle East, into an important aspect of his art. Both Rossetti and Burne-Jones used watercolour to a considerable extent, and their watercolours form an important part of their artistic output.

Watercolour artists in England have always laboured under a feeling of inferiority to painters in oils. It was this impulse that led to the founding in 1804 of the first society specifically for watercolourists, the Old Watercolour Society or OWS. Its members felt that only by establishing their own society, with its own annual exhibitions, could they counter the indifference and hostility of the Royal Academy towards watercolours. Later in the century it became the Royal Watercolour Society, and its members styled themselves RWS. By 1832, the Old Watercolour Society was itself accused of being too exclusive, too conservative, and too commercial, and a rival society was formed, the New Watercolour Society. In 1863 it changed its name to the Royal Institute of Painters in Watercolours, and its members styled themselves RI.

The rivalry between the two societies remained strong throughout the whole of the Victorian period. The OWS tended to attract the more conservative, old-fashioned artists, particularly landscape painters. Samuel Palmer for example, was a member and regular exhibitor. The OWS also favoured the pure watercolour tradition, and was in general opposed to the use of Chinese White, or bodycolour, as it is generally known (see p.110). Helen Allingham, although she did use some bodycolour on occasion, was a traditionalist in matters of technique, and she too belonged to the RWS. The RI tended to attract not only those who used bodycolour, and the stipple technique, such as John Sherrin, but also artists who preferred literary, historical and other more dramatic subjects. For example, Edward Henry Corbould (Plate 13), Historical Painter to Queen Victoria, doubtless felt that his watercolours were a little too unconventional for the RWS, and he therefore patronised the RI. Sir John Gilbert, however, also a painter of romantic, historical subjects (Colour Plate 47), preferred the RWS, and became its President in 1871. It is, therefore, extremely difficult to draw a clear line between the two societies.

By the 1860s, the OWS and the RI could not accommodate the growing demand for exhibition space from young and unknown watercolourists. This led, in 1865, to the founding of the Dudley Gallery. The exhibitions at the Dudley were open to all, and it proved an immediate success, both with younger artists and amateurs. It especially attracted the artists of the incipient Aesthetic Movement, such as Walter Crane and Robert Bateman. The popularity of the Dudley was overshadowed in 1877 by the founding of the bigger and more glamorous Grosvenor Gallery. This had a separate room for watercolours, and in the winter of 1880-1 the gallery held a winter exhibition devoted to contemporary watercolours. Many of the leading artists of the day, such as Burne-Jones, Crane, Tissot, Whistler and Albert Moore, were attracted to the Grosvenor, with the result that the Dudley Gallery amalgamated with the RI in 1881.

There were yet more places a watercolourist could exhibit in the late nineteenth century. Many dealers, such as the Fine Art Society and Agnews, held regular exhibitions, and the Burlington Fine Arts Club often held memorial exhibitions of distinguished watercolourists. In Scotland the Royal Scottish Society of Painters in Watercolours (RSW) was founded in 1878, and there were many other provincial centres where watercolours could be shown. Watercolour was particularly the realm of lady painters, who had their own Society of Lady Artists, though they mostly preferred to exhibit alongside the men.

By the end of the century, the debate over the relative importance of oil and watercolour had died down. Although oils were usually more expensive than

Plate 13. **EDWARD HENRY CORBOULD.** After Dinner

watercolours, and still are, both mediums were seen as of equal artistic importance, and it was during the Victorian period, therefore, that watercolour painting in England came of age.

Teachers and Schools

Watercolour painting, unlike oils, does not require a studio or the purchase of a large amount of equipment. In 1853 Rowneys produced a simple box of watercolours for one shilling (5p), thus making watercolours available to almost all classes of society. As result, watercolour painting became more generally popular in the nineteenth century than at any time in history. The numbers of professionals increased, and so did the numbers of amateurs. The Victorians used their sketchbooks like diaries, endlessly noting and recording all they saw, not only in England, but all over the world; indeed, almost every family in the United Kingdom must contain at least one Victorian ancestor who dabbled in watercolours. It was the perfect medium of expression for the Victorian need to codify, to record, and to comprehend the physical world. It was a profoundly materialistic and scientific age, and the spirit of the age is nowhere better reflected than in its passion for watercolour.

There were numerous art schools and academies where oil painting could be studied,

Plate 14.
**JAMES DUFFIELD
HARDING.**
Lyon from the River

Plate 15.
SAMUEL PROUT.
L'Hotel de Ville, Brussels

but virtually none for watercolourists. Leigh's, which later became Heatherley's Art School, was a private academy where watercolour painting was encouraged. Often artists banded together in informal sketching clubs, to exchange ideas, and compare each other's work. The most usual way to learn watercolour was to take lessons from a professional. For many watercolourists, giving lessons to younger artists, or to amateurs, provided a welcome source of income. Ruskin, who was himself an accomplished watercolourist, took lessons from J.D. Harding (Plate 14), became one of the most enthusiastic supporters of watercolour, and devoted much of his time to writing about it, and reviewing exhibitions. In his *Notes on Samuel Prout and William Hunt* (1879-80) he summed up the appeal of watercolours to the Victorian middle classes:

It is especially to be remembered that drawings of this simple character were made for these same middle classes exclusively . . . the great people always bought Canaletto, not Prout (Plate 15), and Van Huysum, not Hunt. There was indeed no quality in the bright little watercolours which could look other than pert in ghostly corridors, and petty halls of state, but they gave an unquestionable tone of liberal mindedness to a suburban villa, and were the cheerfullest possible decorations for a moderate sized breakfast-parlour opening on a nicely mown lawn.

Colour Plate 48. **JOSEPH MALLORD WILLIAM TURNER.** The Entrance to the Grand Canal

Colour Plate 49. **JOSEPH MALLORD WILLIAM TURNER.** Florence

Technique

At the beginning of the nineteenth century a revolution occurred in watercolour technique which was to have a profound influence on the whole direction of Victorian watercolour painting. This was the introduction of Chinese White, which became available as a manufactured pigment in 1834. Watercolourists quickly found that by mixing Chinese White with their ordinary watercolour pigments, they were able to achieve much greater range, brilliancy and depth of colour. They were also able to paint in much more minute detail, by using small brushes, and a stippling technique, building up the picture by the use of small dots and touches, rather than the broad washes of traditional watercolour. Watercolours mixed with Chinese White had a thicker, more gouache-like appearance, depending on how much white was added. Artists, and art historians, generally describe it as 'bodycolour', which has led to a great deal of confusion. What bodycolour means, quite simply, is that Chinese White has been used to some degree, either mixed in with watercolours, or as white 'highlights', in other words, touches of pure white. Landscape artists found bodycolour particularly useful when painting clouds.

From the beginning, the use of Chinese White, or bodycolour, aroused fierce controversy, and continues to do so even today. Old-fashioned collectors and connoisseurs supported the traditional technique of building up a composition by thin, transparent washes on white paper. The devotees of bodycolour argued that it was an improvement, if properly used, and it was useless to ignore it. Ruskin was a supporter of bodycolour, and in *The Elements of Drawing* (1857) wrote that it 'is just as legitimate as oil-painting, being, so far as handling is concerned, the same process, only without its uncleanliness, its unwholesomeness, or its inconvenience.'

Whether one needed bodycolour or not therefore became a matter of temperament and aesthetic choice. David Cox and his followers clung to the traditional methods; others, such as William Henry Hunt, Birket Foster, and John Frederick Lewis, enthusiastically embraced the possibilities of the new medium. The Pre-Raphaelite Brotherhood and their followers, as might be expected, were all users of bodycolour. Although the Old Watercolour Society tended towards conservatism, many of its members and regular exhibitors used bodycolour, such as W.H. Hunt, J.F. Lewis and Samuel Palmer. The RI and the Dudley by no means had a monopoly on the use of bodycolour; it runs right across the Victorian artistic spectrum. As Kate Greenaway wrote in a letter to Ruskin in 1896, everyone seemed to decry the use of bodycolour, yet 'all the great watercolour people (the modern ones) have used it – W. Hunt, Walker, Pinwell, Rossetti, Burne-Jones, Herkomer.'

In the eighteenth and early nineteenth centuries, watercolour was thought of as the ideal medium for sketching. It enabled an artist to jot down immediate impressions, in a fast and spontaneous manner. Turner is the perfect example of this technique; he filled literally hundreds of sketchbooks with studies of landscape, sea and cloud studies, and topographical views (Colour Plates 48 and 49). Although many nineteenth century artists, both professional and amateur, used watercolour in this way, the tendency in the Victorian period was towards ever-larger, more highly-

Plate 16. **WILLIAM LAKE PRICE.** The Interior of a Gothic Chapel

finished watercolours. Victorian artists favoured the 'exhibition' watercolour, usually displayed in a gold mount and heavy gold frame. This was a deliberate attempt to rival oil paintings, which tended to dominate exhibitions, especially at the Royal Academy. Indeed, a large, highly-finished Victorian watercolour, in its original frame, can look very like an oil painting, and certainly has the same impact on a wall (Plate 16).

As the century advanced, watercolourists used ever-more complex techniques to get the exact effects they wanted. Artists such as John William North and Albert Goodwin exploited the full range of techniques available – not only bodycolour, but also stippling, sponging, and scratching out. The use of bodycolour was often combined with gum arabic, a varnish that gave a similar finish to oil painting. The production of paper also improved during this period, and it became steadily cheaper. A Victorian artist not only had a wide range of colours to choose from, but also papers of different textures and colours.The preparation of the paper was also important, and many artists developed their own ingenious methods. During the Victorian period, watercolour painting reached levels of virtuosity that have never been equalled since.

Colour Plate 50. **THOMAS MILES RICHARDSON, Jnr.** Cowhill Fair, Newcastle

The Early Victorians

By the 1840s, the diversity of styles, techniques and ideas in watercolours was already becoming apparent. Older artists continued to use traditional methods and subject matter; at the same time, a new generation was enthusiastically developing the new techniques available, and expanding the range of subjects.

The tradition of romantic landscapes was still very much alive in the 1840s. Turner, David Cox and Copley Fielding were all still working; John Varley died in 1842, and even Peter De Wint did not die until 1849. All these artists enjoyed immense prestige at the time, and their works would be found in almost any Victorian collection of watercolours. Turner was admired and respected by other artists but, with the exception of Copley Fielding, few attempted to follow in his footsteps. His experiments with colour completely mystified his contemporaries, and were not appreciated until years after his death. In 1843 Ruskin published his celebrated defence of Turner in the first volume of *Modern Painters*. This may have increased Turner's fame and reputation, but it did little to offer artistic direction to younger artists. Turner inspired awe, but few felt able to emulate him. When they did, in the words of Alfred William Rich, it was 'a cause of stumbling and disaster'. Copley Fielding (1787-1855) was one of the very few to do so successfully. His large seascapes and landscapes can be both effective and dramatic, and were lavishly praised by Ruskin (Plate 18). Fielding was President of the RWS from 1831 to 1855, and a highly popular drawing master.

Another RWS stalwart was William Callow, who exhibited nearly 1,400 works there. As a young man Callow had lived in Paris, working as a drawing master (Plate 17). His own watercolour style owes much to the romantic, topographical tradition of

Colour Plate 51. **DAVID COX.** Haddon Hall, Derbyshire

Richard Bonington and Thomas Shotter Boys, who had both lived in Paris. In 1841, Callow returned to London, and in 1848 he became a full member of the RWS. From 1866 to 1870 he was its secretary and for many years exhibited his English and European views there, always maintaining a high degree of professional competence. His watercolours are fresh, and brightly coloured, well-composed, and full of

Plate 17.
WILLIAM CALLOW.
View from the Terrace at
Versailles

Plate 18. **ANTHONY VANDYKE COPLEY FIELDING.** Shoreham, Kent

picturesque groups of figures. At times they can seem a little predictable, even mannered, and as Callow grew older, his work must have seemed increasingly out of date to the mid-Victorians. Probably to compensate for this, Callow also took up oil painting. He long outlived all his contemporaries, and survived into the twentieth century, dying in 1908. Another artist who studied with Bonington, and worked in the same tradition as Shotter Boys and Callow, was William Wyld

William Leighton Leitch, on the other hand, supported the RI of which he was Vice-President for many years. Leitch began his career in Glasgow as a theatrical scenery painter, like two other northerners, David Roberts (Plate 19), and Clarkson Stanfield. He then took up both oil painting and watercolour, but it is as a watercolourist that he will be chiefly remembered, because he was watercolour teacher to Queen Victoria and the Royal Family for many years. Leitch was a skilled and competent landscape painter and topographer (Plate 20), and there are numbers of his works in the Royal Collection, mainly views of Osborne, Balmoral and Rosenau, Prince Albert's birthplace. Another artist to enjoy royal favour was Joseph Nash. He trained as an architectural draughtsman under A.C. Pugin, specialising in Gothic and Elizabethan buildings (Plate 21). He also worked in Paris, and his style falls into the Bonington-Shotter Boys-Callow tradition. He became best known for his architectural books, including, *Views of Windsor Castle* (1848) and *The Mansions of England In the Olden Time* (1839-49). The latter is full of grand interiors of Tudor and Elizabethan buildings with figures in brightly coloured costumes of the period. They typify the romantic, historical taste of the 1840s. Nash is better known today, however, for his views of the Crystal Palace, which enjoyed a wide circulation through coloured lithographs. These are some of the finest views of the Great

Plate 19. **DAVID ROBERTS.** Christian and Mohammedan Churches on the Summit of Sinai

Exhibition, particularly the interiors and studies of the individual stands. A great number of the original watercolours are in the Royal Collection.

In the early Victorian period, there were still many landscape artists and topographers working in the provinces. Typical of the breed was Thomas Miles Richardson, Senior, of Newcastle-Upon-Tyne. He was born in 1784, and therefore belongs more to the romantic period. He painted both oils and watercolours, chiefly views of his native north-east, in a fresh and lively style. Some of his larger watercolours can be extremely dramatic and romantic, and his work is still much prized among northern collectors. Richardson died in 1848, and several of his sons were artists. The best of them, and the one who most closely imitated his style was Thomas Miles Richardson, Junior (Colour Plate 50). He travelled further afield than his father, in Scotland and on the Continent, eventually settling in London. His later works, especially his Italian views, are bright and pleasing, with plenty of blue sky and plenty of Chinese White, though with a tendency to the formulaic. Another family specialising in similar views were the Rowbothams; in particular Thomas Charles Leeson Rowbotham, and his son Charles, both of whom spent a lifetime catering to the almost limitless Victorian appetite for picturesque views of Italy.

Much more influential was David Cox, Senior, who is still regarded today as one of the masters of the traditional watercolour (Colour Plate 51). He published several books on watercolour painting, which were widely read at the time, and exhibited regularly at the OWS from 1813 until his death in 1859. His early style was tight and topographical, but as he grew older he gradually broadened his technique, becoming almost an Impressionist in his later years. His rendering of broad, windswept landscapes, and racing clouds, often painted on a rough, textured paper

Colour Plate 52. **SAMUEL PALMER.** Illustration to Milton's *Lycidas*

for greater effect, was widely admired, and imitated, throughout the Victorian period. Thomas Collier and Edmund Wimperis were among his many followers, carrying on the Cox tradition to the end of the century. His son, David Cox, Junior, also closely imitated his father's style, which has led to endless confusion between the two. There are also numerous fakes and forgeries in circulation, which testify to the very considerable reputation which Cox enjoyed in the Victorian period. Cox's style was rugged, realistic, and down-to-earth, but hardly romantic, except in its glorification of the English landscape. His affinities are more with Constable than with Turner.

Another landscape watercolourist of the early Victorian period was Samuel Palmer. He too was a member of the RWS, and a regular exhibitor there. Yet his approach to landscape could hardly be more different from that of Cox. He was an unashamed visionary and romantic, whose landscapes aim to convey a poetic mood, rather than depict any particular scene. As a young man, Palmer had fallen under the spell of William Blake. From 1826 to 1835 he lived at Shoreham in Kent, and it was during this celebrated 'Shoreham period' that he painted some of the most mystical and intense landscapes of English art. In 1835 he moved to London, married John Linnell's daughter, Hannah, in 1837, and then spent two years in Italy. Palmer died in 1881, so the rest of his career belongs to the Victorian period. His later works are highly-wrought and intensely colourful, with liberal use of bodycolour and gum arabic. Although quite different from the almost monochrome austerity of his Shoreham works, these later landscapes by Palmer still have a vivid intensity quite different from most of his contemporaries. His skies and his sunsets glow with a mystical radiance that no other Victorian watercolourist could equal (Colour Plate 52).

Colour Plate 53.
WILLIAM HENRY HUNT. Bird's Nest and Blossom

Colour Plate 54.
JOHN SHERRIN.
Bird's Nest and Blossom

Like the Pre-Raphaelites, Palmer worked over a board prepared with a white background to give his colours the richness of tone that he wanted.

Although the RWS is generally thought of as more conservative, two of its members and exhibitors were the most innovative watercolourists of the 1840s – William Henry Hunt and John Frederick Lewis. Hunt began his career as a painter and pupil of John Varley. His early works were painted in the broad manner of his master, Varley, but during the 1830s, he took up the use of bodycolour, and completely changed his style. At the same time, he began to paint the fruit and flower studies for which he is now best known. These small, intensely coloured, minutely observed studies of fruit, blossom and birds' nests are perhaps the most quintessentially Victorian of all watercolours (Colour Plate 53). For Ruskin, they were more than just studies, they were models of how nature should be painted. Endless artists, both professional and amateur, not only imitated Hunt's subjects, but also his microscopic, stippled technique, using opaque bodycolour over a white background. Among his numerous followers were John Sherrin (Colour Plate 54), William Hough (Colour Plate 55), William Cruikshank, T.F. Collier, and the three Clares – George, Oliver and Vincent. Ruskin wrote copiously and often about Hunt, and no Victorian collection was complete without at least one of his bird's nests.

Plate 20. **WILLIAM LEIGHTON LEITCH.** On Lake Maggiore

Plate 21. **JOSEPH NASH.** The Drawing Room, Ashton Hall, Warwickshire

Thackeray was also an admirer, and wrote that if he was a Duke, he would like to have two Hunts in every room in all his houses. Thackeray also greatly admired Hunt's rustic interiors, and his many studies of country children, which he described as 'real' nature, now, real expression, real startling home poetry . . .'

The intense realism of Hunt's interiors of old farm buildings and the figures, must have seemed startlingly modern to the viewer of the 1840s (Colour Plate 56). They had an immense influence on other Victorian watercolourists for the rest of the century, in particular on Birket Foster and Frederick Walker, both themselves highly influential. Hunt was equally good at interiors of grand rooms, too, and frequently painted them when staying at his friend J.H. Maw's house in Hastings.

By the beginning of the Victorian period, John Frederick Lewis was already a well-known watercolourist. Born into an artistic family, he studied animals with the young Edwin Landseer, and turned to watercolours in the 1820s. He travelled widely in Europe, and by 1840 he was already well-known for his colourful views in France, Italy and Spain. Like Hunt, Lewis made copious use of bodycolour, and his watercolours were also brightly coloured, and full of meticulous observation. In 1840 came the turning point in his career, when he decided to travel in Greece and the Middle East. He settled in Cairo for the next ten years, where Thackeray visited him, describing his life-style as 'like a languid lotus-eater – a dreamy, hazy, lazy, tobaccoified life'. But there was nothing hazy or lazy about Lewis's work at this period. Like so many of the Victorians, he became fascinated by Arab life, and it was to inspire his greatest works (Colour Plate 57). When he finally returned to England in 1850, and began to exhibit his watercolours of Arab life, they caused an

Colour Plate 55. **WILLIAM HOUGH.** Apples and Grapes

immediate sensation. The Victorian public was not only intrigued by his detailed observations of an exotic society, but marvelled at the perfection of his jewel-like technique, which seemed perfectly suited to the intense sunlight and brilliant colours of Egyptian life. Many of his watercolours were of harems, or 'Hhareems', which of course lent an added sexual piquancy to the Victorian male viewer in his top hat and frock coat. The faces of his women are deliberately Europeanised, presumably to make them more acceptable to English taste, but they must nonetheless have brought an exotic thrill to any Victorian exhibition. To this day, they are the most highly-prized and expensive of all orientalist watercolours. Many

Plate 22.
AUGUSTUS OSBORNE LAMPLOUGH.
An Arab Warrior on a Camel in the Desert

120

Colour Plate 56. **WILLIAM HENRY HUNT.** Interior of a Barn

other watercolourists visited the Middle East, although they were oil painters as well – David Roberts, Edward Lear, Richard Dadd and Holman Hunt among them (Plate 22). The Pre-Raphaelite technique was anticipated by both William Henry Hunt and J.F. Lewis in the 1840s; what was different about the Pre-Raphaelites was their revolutionary ideas, and their determination to make a break with tradition. Their techniques were not new, rather it was the uses to which they put them.

Colour Plate 57.
JOHN FREDERICK LEWIS.
A Halt in the Desert

Colour Plate 58. **FORD MADOX BROWN.** Elijah and the Widow's Son

Colour Plate 59. **WILLIAM HOLMAN HUNT.** A Wadi in Palestine

The Pre-Raphaelites

Nearly all the members of the Pre-Raphaelite Brotherhood, and their early followers, made use of watercolour, although Millais only used it occasionally to make small replicas of his oils and Arthur Hughes did not use it at all. Both Holman Hunt and Ford Madox Brown used watercolour extensively. In the case of Ford Madox Brown it was mainly to explore themes already developed in his paintings. Thus he made watercolours of both biblical and historical subjects and often made an oil and a watercolour version of the same subject. An example of this is 'Elijah and the Widow's Son' of 1864, which Brown was commissioned to illustrate for the publisher Dalziel's Bible Gallery (Colour Plate 58). With typical thoroughness Brown researched the costumes, the setting and the Christian iconography of the subject, and then tried to depict the scene in a highly realistic and dramatic way. Elijah is shown descending some very steep steps, carrying the young boy, still wrapped in his grave-clothes, while the widow gives thanks on her knees at the foot of the steps. Here Madox Brown has clearly used watercolour as a method of working out his ideas for the composition and the colours before completing the oil. But the watercolour is more than just a study – it is a finished work of art in its own right. In landscape, Madox Brown used watercolour in a similar way. His watercolour 'Hampstead, a Sketch from Nature' of 1877, also known as 'Hampstead from my Window', is another view from the back of his house in Kentish Town, similar to his oil painting of the same subject, 'An English Autumn Afternoon', which he finished about two years earlier. The deliberate choice of an ordinary and unpretentious subject, a suburban landscape, is both typical of Madox Brown, and of the Pre-Raphaelites in the 1850s.

For Holman Hunt, watercolour was a way of recording his travels, especially his three visits to the Holy Land. Hunt's purpose in visiting the Middle East was to study the authentic settings of biblical history, and he described J.F. Lewis dismissively as 'the painter of Egyptian social scenes'. Hunt became fascinated, not only by Judaic history and ritual, but also by the strange and arid landscape. He recorded his impressions of it in numerous watercolours which are among the finest Middle Eastern views by an English artist (Colour Plate 59). In spite of Hunt's determination

Plate 23. **JOHN RILEY WILMER.** The Virgin and Child

to record the scenery in precise detail, these watercolours have an almost hallucinatory effect because of their vivid range of colours, predominantly orange and purple. Similar watercolours by Hunt's companion, Thomas Seddon, show that this was exactly how the landscape did look. Nonetheless, Hunt's watercolours do have an intensity that lifts them above mere realism; in spirit they seem close to Samuel Palmer. Hunt's Italian watercolours have a similarly dramatic quality. So as a watercolourist he really belongs among the Victorian travellers.

Of all the Pre-Raphaelites, it was Rossetti who made the greatest use of watercolour. His watercolours made an important contribution to the Pre-Raphaelite movement and were in no way peripheral or secondary to his oils. Rossetti was never as technically accomplished as Millais or Hunt, but he found watercolour the perfect medium of expression in his early years. Whatever his watercolours may lack in technical finish, they more than make up for in colour, intensity and romantic subject matter (Colour Plate 60). His two most important sources of

Colour Plate 60. **DANTE GABRIEL ROSSETTI.** Lady Lileth

Plate 24. **HENRY MEYNELL RHEAM.** Once upon a Time

inspiration in the 1850s were the poetry of Dante, and *Morte d'Arthur* by Sir Thomas Malory. The story of Dante and Beatrice inspired many of his finest watercolours, such as 'The First Anniversary of the Death of Beatrice (Dante drawing an Angel)' of 1853. Some of his watercolours on the theme of King Arthur, such as 'Arthur's Tomb' of 1854, are among the most remarkable products of the Pre-Raphaelite movement. Small, brightly-coloured and two-dimensional, they glow like jewels and project an intensely romantic vision of the Middle Ages.

Colour Plate 61. **SIR EDWARD BURNE-JONES.** The Annunciation

Plate 25. **HENRY JOHN STOCK.** The Poet's Dream

In 1856, Rossetti met Morris and Burne-Jones, which led to their working together on the murals for the new library of the Oxford Union. Although these have virtually disappeared, many of Rossetti's watercolour versions of them do survive, and, for example, 'How Sir Galahad, Sir Bors and Sir Perceval were fed with the Sanc Grael' (1864) or 'The Wedding of St. George and the Princess Sabra' (1857) are among his finest works. James Smetham described the latter as 'one of the grandest things, like a golden dim dream. Love "credulous all gold", gold armour, a sense of secret enclosure in "palace chambers far apart".' Also in the 1850s, Rossetti explored one or two musical subjects, such as 'The Blue Closet' of 1857, which although medieval, are deliberately subject-less and anticipate the theories of the Aesthetic Movement. After the death of Elizabeth Siddal in 1862, Rossetti worked increasingly in oils and on a larger scale. But for many, his early watercolours are the quintessential pre-Raphaelite pictures.

Like Rossetti, Burne-Jones particularly used watercolours at the beginning of his career. At this period he was also painting Arthurian subjects which continued to inspire him for the rest of his career. 'The Madness of Sir Tristram' of 1862, for

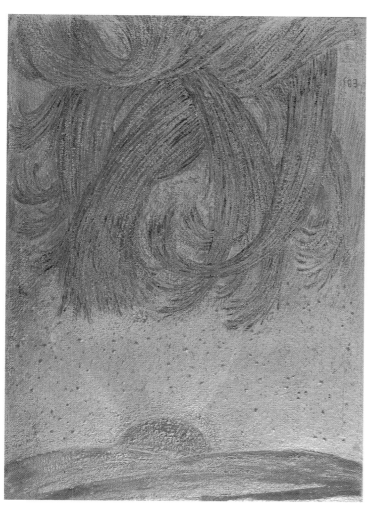

Colour Plate 62.
SIR EDWARD BURNE-JONES.
Sunset and Corn

Plate 26.
THOMAS MATTHEW ROOKE.
A Lych Gate

Colour Plate 63. **JOHN RODDAM SPENCER-STANHOPE.** The Washing Place

example, is a scene from *Morte d'Arthur,* showing Sir Tristram, driven to madness by his love for Iseult, living in the forest as a herdsman. As so often with Burne-Jones, the idea for the watercolour came out of his design work for Morris & Co., in this case a set of stained glass panels. By this time Burne-Jones was also making use of bodycolour and coloured chalks to achieve a richer, more old-masterish tone. He had already visited Italy twice, and the influence of the Italian Renaissance clearly begins to show in his watercolours of the 1860s. 'Green Summer', another watercolour of 1864, has echoes of both Botticelli and Giorgione in its romantic mood, although the green colouring belongs more to the Aesthetic Movement. It shows just how Burne-Jones was evolving his own very personal fusion between Pre-Raphaelitism and the Italian Renaissance (Colour Plate 61).

Classical influences are also detectable in Burne-Jones's work during the 1860s, and he attempted several mythological subjects. One of these, 'Phyllis and Demophoon', of 1870, caused a furor when he exhibited it at the OWS. Taken from Ovid's *Heroides*, it shows the two lovers embracing at the moment when Phyllis is turned into an almond tree. In spite of its respectable classical theme, and highly stylised treatment of romantic love, the critics strongly objected to the nudity of the male figure. Burne-Jones responded by withdrawing the watercolour from the exhibition and resigning his membership. Until the opening of the Grosvenor Gallery in 1877, he did not exhibit again in public.

From the 1870s onwards, Burne-Jones working increasingly in oil, and on a larger and larger scale. But he never gave up watercolour and continued to use it for smaller works, landscapes, figure and composition studies. He also used it in much of his design work. For Burne-Jones, watercolour was a way of developing and working out his ideas (Colour Plate 62). Many of his portraits and studies of heads are also in watercolour. In all these works, Burne-Jones made great use of bodycolour, sometimes to the extent that it is difficult to say whether a work is in oil or in watercolour. As a result, they are often described as gouache, implying a deliberate mixture between thin oil and watercolour. Whistler mocked Burne-Jones

Colour Plate 64. **EVELYN DE MORGAN.** Hero

for this during the Whistler v. Ruskin trial, claiming that Burne-Jones did not know the difference between oil and watercolour. This was an unfair accusation. Burne-Jones's technique was a kind of half-way house between the two, but it suited his romantic, dreamy style perfectly, and was imitated by many of his followers (Plates 23, 24 and 25). Evelyn De Morgan (Colour Plate 64), and her uncle John Roddam Spencer-Stanhope (Colour Plate 63), both used gouache and watercolour in a similar way to Burne-Jones. Many of Simeon Solomon's finest biblical works of the 1860s are his watercolours (Colour Plate 65).

There were many other followers of Burne-Jones in the 1870s and 1880s, and many of them used watercolour, as well as oil. T.M. Rooke, who was Burne-Jones's studio assistant, used watercolour, especially when painting topographical views of old buildings on the Continent (Plate 26). Walter Crane and Robert Bateman both

Colour Plate 65. **SIMEON SOLOMON.** Shadrach, Meshak, and Abednego in the Fiery Furnace

Colour Plate 66. **JOHN BYAM SHAW.** Diana of the Hunt

painted in watercolour, especially for romantic, moody landscapes, in a similar vein to those of Burne-Jones. Later in the century, both Byam Shaw (Colour Plate 66) and Eleanor Fortescue-Brickdale (Frontispiece) made use of watercolour for literary and historical subjects. Both artists worked as book illustrators, as did numerous late Victorian artists. Many illustrators of this period were also accomplished watercolourists, such as Kate Greenaway, Randolph Caldecott, Arthur Rackham and Edmund Dulac. Although they belong to the history of illustration, their contribution to the art of watercolour should not be overlooked.

Plate 27.
WILLIAM BELL SCOTT.
Hexham Market Place,
Northumberland

Plate 28. **JOHN BRETT.** The Castle of Joree

Colour Plate 67. **JOHN RUSKIN.** Baden, Switzerland

Pre-Raphaelite Landscape

It was in the realm of landscape painting that the Pre-Raphaelite movement was to have its greatest influence on watercolourists. Among landscape painters in oil, the Pre-Raphaelite influence was already on the wane during the 1860s. But among watercolour artists, its influence proved to be much more pervasive and long-lasting. Some watercolourists continued to use Pre-Raphaelite techniques right up to the end of the century, even though their subject matter might be very different.

The teachings of Ruskin had even greater relevance for watercolourists than for oil painters, particularly as Ruskin himself was an enthusiastic and highly competent watercolourist. His insistence on the microscopic approach to landscape, combined with a mystical reverence for all nature, naturally lent itself to the new Victorian technique of watercolour combined with bodycolour, especially when combined with the stippling method. In his *Elements of Drawing* of 1857, Ruskin suggested that 'in general, all banks are beautiful things, and will reward work better than large landscapes.' He also encouraged artists to study the edges of rivers, with old posts, or roots of trees; roadsides, especially in chalk country; tree trunks, especially those with wild flowers or ivy growing up them. Many Victorian artists obliged with watercolours of precisely these subjects. Ruskin himself made similar studies, especially of lichen-covered rocks, reflecting his botanical and geological interests. He also made many wonderful studies of architectural details (Colour Plate 67). When it came to landscape, he was not as good at following his own precepts, using broader washes inspired by his great hero, Turner.

One of Ruskin's particular obsessions was the recording of architectural details of old buildings, especially in Venice. This was an activity that suited the Pre-Raphaelite

Colour Plate 68. **GEORGE PRICE BOYCE.** Streatley Mill at Sunset

style and numerous artists followed his example, including G.P. Boyce, who visited Italy in 1854. Ruskin's own studies in Venice are among his finest works. By 1878 he was financially independent enough to found his own Guild of St. George, which was effectively a private museum devoted to acquiring and commissioning the kind of art he liked. The best artist to work for the Guild was John Wharlton Bunney, who lived in Venice from 1869 until his death in 1882. Under Ruskin's influence he painted a number of meticulous, but rather lifeless watercolours of Venice, thus revealing the strengths, and the weaknesses, of the Pre-Raphaelite style. One was a large view of St. Mark's Basilica which took him twelve years to paint. Ruskin also bought Italian views by the American watercolourist, Henry Roderick Newman.

Most of the close followers of the Pre-Raphaelite Brotherhood used watercolour to some degree. William Bell Scott (Plate 27), the Newcastle painter and poet, used watercolour not only for highly detailed landscapes, but also for more ambitious, historical and biblical scenes. John Brett (Plate 28) occasionally used watercolour to record views of coastal towns. John William Inchbold, the Leeds artist, used watercolour considerably more often. Both Brett and Inchbold were subjected to advice and encouragement from Ruskin, who travelled with both of them. Although Inchbold's paintings are strictly Pre-Raphaelite and Ruskinian, his watercolours reveal a lighter and broader touch that is more akin to the Aesthetic Movement (Plate 29). His delicate style is seen at its best in his many watercolours of the Alps. William Henry

Plate 29. **JOHN WILLIAM INCHBOLD.** Greenwich, London

Millais, brother of the more famous John Everett, used watercolour considerably better than his illustrious brother. During the 1850s and 1860s, he produced seascape and landscape studies in an intensely Pre-Raphaelite style. His studies of bracken and woodland plants are particularly well observed (Plate 31). Frederick Sandys, one of the most technically accomplished of all the Pre-Raphaelites, mainly worked in oil or pastel, but he did produce a small number of brilliant watercolour landscapes.

Two of the most interesting watercolourists on the fringe of the Pre-Raphaelite movement were George Price Boyce and Alfred William Hunt. Boyce was a friend and neighbour of Rossetti in Chelsea as well as a friend of Ruskin, and his diaries are an important source of information about Pre-Raphaelite circles. He exhibited at the RWS, becoming a full member in 1877. Boyce applied the landscape principles of Ruskin more rigorously than most of the other artists, but did so in a highly distinctive and individual way. He often chose deliberately unremarkable landscapes, but depicted them in a way that made them remarkable by means of colouring, intense observation and composition. He liked old buildings, and often incorporated them in his landscapes, almost always choosing a surprising perspective or odd point of view. Although eccentric, his watercolours are completely individual, and instantly recognisable, both by their subject matter and their distinctive technique (Colour Plate 68).

Alfred William Hunt won the Newdigate Prize for English Verse at Oxford in 1851 and was a fellow at Oxford University until 1861, when he married and decided to devote himself to art as a career. He had already exhibited at the Liverpool Academy in the 1850s where he became a member in 1856. In 1862 he came to London, and began to exhibit at the RWS of which he became a member in 1864. Hunt's landscape watercolours represent another very personal interpretation of Pre-Raphaelite ideas. They are brightly coloured and full of detail, but they also have a

Colour Plate 69 **ALBERT GOODWIN.** A Mountain Stream

Colour Plate 70. **MYLES BIRKET FOSTER.** The Itinerant Fiddler

Colour Plate 71. **RICHARD REDGRAVE.** Parkhurst Woods, Abinger, Surrey

feeling of light and an atmospheric softness that sets them apart from the general run of Pre-Raphaelite watercolours (Plate 30). He painted in Scotland, the Lakes and the Thames Valley, but was particularly fond of North Wales and Whitby. He also travelled in France and Switzerland. Thanks to numerous northern friends and patrons, he was also encouraged to paint occasional industrial subjects, such as the remarkable 'Travelling Cranes, Diving Bell etc. on the unfinished Part of Tynemouth Pier'. Hunt was one of many Victorian watercolourists to experiment with papers, colours and techniques. His daughter Violet Hunt, author of *The Wife of Rossetti*, described how her father 'delicately stained pieces of Whatman's Imperial . . . to the most murderous "process" . . . he sponged them into submission; he scraped them into rawness and a fresh state of receptivity.' In this respect he was similar to another great Victorian watercolourist, also a protégé of Ruskin, Albert Goodwin (Colour Plate 69). In the 1860s Goodwin had been a pupil of both Arthur Hughes and Madox Brown. He also fell under the spell of Ruskin, who took him to Italy in 1872. He had what might therefore be described as a complete Pre-Raphaelite education, and his early watercolours reflect this. Later, however, his style developed away from Pre-Raphaelitism, and his career belongs more properly among the Victorian travellers.

Many other watercolourists fell under the spell of the Pre-Raphaelites in the 1850s and 1860s. The movement inspired some to paint their finest works; for others it was just a passing artistic phase, before they moved on to something else. Richard Redgrave, the pioneer of social realist subjects in the 1840s, turned to landscapes in the 1850s which he painted both in oil and watercolour. His watercolour landscapes, mostly painted near his house at Abinger in Surrey, are brilliant essays in the Pre-Raphaelite style (Colour Plate 71).

Much the same could be said of Edmund George Warren, who specialised in woodland subjects. His rendering of old trees, undergrowth and leaves is technically astonishing at its best, and pushed the Pre-Raphaelite landscape style to its utmost limits (Colour Plate 73). Ruskin, with typical perversity, criticised Warren's landscapes as too mechanical. Discouraged, Warren broadened his style, and turned to painting landscapes instead of woodlands, usually scenes involving a harvest field. Warren was a regular exhibitor, and member, at the RI. The career of George Shalders followed much the same route as that of Warren. In the 1850s under Pre-Raphaelite influence, he produced landscapes of exceptional brilliance. Later he turned to more humdrum country scenes with cattle and sheep, which are often attractive but lack that Pre-Raphaelite magic (Colour Plate 72). John George Sowerby, a little-known Newcastle artist, produced a small number of landscapes and garden scenes which show a genuine Pre-Raphaelite intensity of vision (Plate 32). His daughter was the watercolourist, Millicent Sowerby, whose works are in a similar vein to those of Kate Greenaway.

Henry Clarence Whaite was another landscape watercolourist perversely

Plate 30. **ALFRED WILLIAM HUNT.** Time and Tide

Plate 31. **WILLIAM HENRY MILLAIS.** Woodland Steps

141

Colour Plate 72. **GEORGE SHALDERS.** The Shepherd Boy

criticised by Ruskin for following those very principles that Ruskin himself advocated. Whaite in fact produced some very remarkable landscape watercolours, especially of Wales and the Lake District, but Ruskin wrote that Whaite was 'suffering under the . . . oppression of plethoric labour.' On another occasion he wrote that 'the execution of the whole by minute and similar touches is a mistake.' It was these contradictions that eventually led Ruskin to give up supporting the Pre-Raphaelite style, and stop writing his annual *Academy Notes* in 1859.

Plate 32. **JOHN GEORGE SOWERBY.** Flowers by a Rocky Stream

Colour Plate 73. **EDMUND GEORGE WARREN.** Lost in the Woods

Plate 33. **ARTHUR SEVERN.** Old Hungerford Bridge, Chelsea

The Aesthetic Movement

The Aesthetic Movement affected watercolour artists just as much as it affected painters in oil, but given the nature of the medium, its influence was somewhat different. As in painting, the Aesthetic Movement was a reaction against the doctrines that had held sway during the Pre-Raphaelite domination of the 1850s and 1860s, and against the artistic and moral straightjacket of the Ruskinian philosophy. The movement was a move towards a wider and more eclectic range of subjects, towards poetry and imagination rather than the mere transcription of reality (Plate 33). In watercolour, it also encouraged a wider range of techniques, as artists searched for a medium suited to the expression of their artistic ideas.

Watercolour artists adapted to the Aesthetic Movement in a wide variety of ways. Many of the younger artists of the 1860s had worked as illustrators, designing woodblocks for use in magazines and books. This often affected their style when they came to use watercolour. A typical example of this is the work of Birket Foster, who was arguably the best known and most successful of all Victorian watercolourists. Foster began his career as a wood engraver. At first he produced illustrations for magazines, such as *Punch* and *The Illustrated London News.* Then he turned to book illustration and about 1859 took up watercolour painting. Foster brought the sharpness and minuteness of an engraver's eye to bear on the medium of watercolour. Like the Pre-Raphaelites, he worked over a white ground, using very small brushes and a stipple technique, similar to that of William Henry Hunt, whose works he admired and collected. Like Hunt, he tended to fill up the whole of the picture space with equal intensity, giving his watercolours an all-over brightness. In the wrong hands, this technique can look artificial and over-laboured.

Plate 34.
**JOHN WILLIAM
NORTH.**
A Woodland Spring

Birket Foster was enough of a technician to master it; many of his pupils could not.

Birket Foster may have used the techniques of the Pre-Raphaelites but when he came to depict country life, his approach was very different. He was not interested in grappling with social problems, or depicting the evils of the countryside. As a hard-headed northerner who had made his own way, he knew that merry England was what sold, not misery England. His watercolours project an image of a rural paradise, and they struck a deep chord in the Victorian psyche. Foster's delightful visions of the English countryside, with their picturesque cottages, happy villagers and cheerful

Colour Plate 74. **MYLES BIRKET FOSTER.** Boys Fishing from a Punt

children, portray a lost Eden that never really existed at any period, they but are still the most enduringly popular images of England (Colour Plate 74). The Victorians loved them, and a successful businessman with any pretensions to aesthetic taste had to own one. Their appeal has remained constant to this day, even through the darkest days of modernism, and postcards of them are sold all over the world.

From the start, Birket Foster supported the OWS. He became a member in 1862, exhibiting over four hundred watercolours there. By 1863 he was already doing well enough to build his own house at Witley, Surrey. Here he gathered around him a colony of fellow-artists, including Fred Walker and Helen Allingham, and collected the works of the Pre-Raphaelites, specially Burne-Jones. Although Foster is best known for his cottage and village scenes, his range was wider than this and included landscapes, topographical views and coastal scenes. He also travelled on the Continent, in 1868 to Venice with Orchardson and Walker. Birket Foster was not only successful, he was hugely influential, particularly on Fred Walker and the group now known as the Idyllists – John William North, George John Pinwell and Robert Walker Macbeth. At a lower level, many lesser artists followed in his footsteps, right up to the end of the century, repeating his formulas, but rarely equalling his brilliance.

The best of the many followers of Birket Foster was Frederick Walker, who was regarded by many as one of the brightest stars among the young artists of the 1860s (Colour Plate 75). Birket Foster may have been more popular with patrons and collectors but Walker was more admired by critics and his fellow-artists. He was an 'artists' artist'. Like Birket Foster, Walker painted country life, but he was more concerned with social issues. He wanted to portray the reality and the pathos of country life but without appearing gloomy or pessimistic. He also tried to make his figures much more monumental, and as a result they often have a 'posed' look. Walker had also worked as an illustrator in the 1860s, contributing drawings to *Once a Week* and *Cornhill Magazine*, and although he also painted in oil, and

Colour Plate 75. **FREDERICK WALKER.** Strange Faces

exhibited at the RA, it was his watercolours that bought him the greatest success. His simple, yet poetic evocations of country life, such as the much-reproduced 'Spring' in the Victoria andAlbert Museum, were enormously admired by his fellow-artists. Walker made liberal use of Chinese White, and even made a caricature of himself squeezing out a huge tube of it, the caption reading 'What would "The Society" say if it could only see me?' He worked out of doors, like the Pre-Raphaelites, and his work, like theirs, is full of observed detail, but he then worked over it as if to cover up his tracks. 'Composition is the art of preserving the accidental look', he wrote. No artist can have laboured harder to make his watercolours look accidental. Sadly, he died of consumption at the tragically early age of thirty-five. He was buried at Cookham-on-Thames, where many of his pictures were painted, and where Stanley Spencer was to paint very different pictures in the next century.

Walker's close friend John William North shared a very similar artistic training. He too worked for a wood engraver, and produced illustrations for books and magazines. In the 1860s he worked for Dalziel and such magazines as *Good Words* and *The Sunday Magazine.* In 1868 he rented Halsway Court, a beautiful old manor house in Somerset. Here he and his fellow Idyllists found solace and inspiration in the unspoiled Somerset countryside. Walker often stayed there in a search for suitable rural subjects. North himself preferred pure landscape, sometimes asking Walker to paint his figures for him. Like Walker, North painted landscape in an intense and detailed style, particularly concentrating on wild and tangled undergrowth (Plate 34). But he then worked over the surface, producing a shimmering, misty effect which is

Plate 35. **GEORGE JOHN PINWELL.** The Pied Piper of Hamelin

the hallmark of his style. North, too, strove to make his watercolours look accidental, but they are highly contrived, as is all the work of the Idyllists.

The third of the Idyllist triumvirate was George John Pinwell. Yet again, he started life as a wood engraver with the Dalziel Brothers. He then took up watercolours and began to exhibit at the Dudley and the RWS of which he became a member in 1870. Walker, North and Pinwell had studied together at Leigh's Academy, although Walker and Pinwell did not become close friends. Nonetheless, their work is often compared. Pinwell shared North's poetic and romantic feelings for the English countryside, but his figures and compositions are much more elaborate. Pinwell attempted large historical subjects, such as 'Gilbert à Becket's Troth' which was much praised at the RWS in 1872. Pinwell's work of this kind is intensely romantic in feeling, and typical of the aesthetic mood of the 1870s (Plate 35). Although beautiful, they have a tendency to be both theatrical and artificial. More effective are his simpler studies of landscape and country life, which sparkle with brilliant colour and light. Like Walker, Pinwell died tragically young of consumption.

The Idyllists did not form a coherent group, and the name was only applied to them later, in the 1890s, but the term usefully describes the watercolour style prevalent in the 1860s and 1870s, which the critics sarcastically described as the 'poetry without grammar school'. Most of these artists favoured the Dudley Gallery, then later the Grosvenor. Among many others who might be mentioned in this group are Robert Walker Macbeth and Hubert von Herkomer. Both worked for *The Graphic* in the 1860s, and when they came to paint watercolours of country life their work is much tinged with realism. Macbeth's work certainly tries to show country life as it really was (Plate 36), and his watercolours of life in Lincolnshire and Somerset were compared to the works of Thomas Hardy. Herkomer, too, was not afraid to depict poverty and old age in his watercolours. These only formed a small part of his output, for he was mainly an oil painter, but his watercolours are deserving of more attention (Plate 37). Many artists continued to work in the Idyllist style for the rest of the century. Lionel Percy Smythe, for example, was a landscape

Plate 36. **ROBERT WALKER MACBETH.** A Summer's Day by the Millpond

Plate 37. **HUBERT von HERKOMER.** A Weary Way

Colour Plate 76. **KATE GREENAWAY.** Through the White Flowers

and figurative artist who lived latterly in northern France. His work has a delicacy and refinement that recalls the Idyllists and his figures often echo those of Walker.

Next to Birket Foster, the most popular and now the best known of the Idyllists is Helen Allingham whose huge popularity is based on her watercolours of picturesque old cottages, which enjoy almost world-wide fame through reproductions and cards. Born Helen Paterson, she studied at the RA schools, becoming a regular exhibitor at the RWS and a member by 1890. In 1874 she married the impoverished Irish poet William Allingham, and her watercolours provided the family with a vital source of income. Through her husband she met Carlyle, Tennyson and Ruskin, who became a great admirer of her work. In 1881 she and her family moved out of London to the Surrey village of Witley near Haslemere. Here she was a near neighbour of Birket Foster, and there is no doubt that she admired his work as well as that of Fred Walker and to some extent imitated their subjects. But she made the painting of old cottages her own particular speciality (Colour Plate 77). People think that Allingham's cottages are sentimental, but her purpose in painting them was as much preservationist as artistic. She knew that they represented a vanishing way of life and was determined to record it before it was too late. Her watercolours are therefore not so much sentimental as nostalgic. They are in a way the visual equivalent of the writings of Flora Thompson, who was also describing a way of life that was rapidly disappearing.

Allingham's technique was wonderfully soft and delicate, and she made sparing

Colour Plate 77. **HELEN ALLINGHAM.** Cottage at Brook, near Witley, Surrey

Plate 38 .
**CHARLES EDWARD
WILSON.**
A Difficult Problem

use of bodycolour. Compared to the delicacy and subtlety of Allingham, Birket Foster's cottage scenes can seem quite garish. Her range of subjects was much wider than just cottages. She painted landscapes and country scenes, gardens, interiors and portraits, and also visited Venice. She illustrated three books, *The Cottage Homes of England*, *Happy England* and *The Gardens of Tennyson*, all of which are now collectors' items. Ruskin wrote in *The Art of England* (1884) of her skill at capturing 'the gesture, character and humour of charming children in country landscapes.' In the same book Ruskin linked her work with that of another lady watercolourist, Kate Greenaway, whose work really belongs among the

Plate 39. **JOHN ANSTER FITZGERALD.** The Fairy Falconer

illustrators, but she was a friend and sketching companion of Helen Allingham, and her delightful figures of girls in Regency dresses and mob caps were enormously popular in the 1870s and 1880s and formed an essential ingredient of the Aesthetic Movement (Colour Plate 76). Most of her watercolours and drawings are small, and relate to illustrations for her books.

Birket Foster and Allingham had many imitators, particularly of the 'cottage door' variety, but few equals. Among the better practitioners of this genre were Arthur Claude Strachan (Colour Plate 78), Henry John Johnstone, Ethel Hughes, William Affleck and Charles Edward Wilson (Plate 38). The cottage hearth was an almost equally popular subject, and some artists made a speciality of this, such as Carlton Alfred Smith, and Henry Spernon Tozer.

The Victorians firmly believed in fairies, and the fairy painters have already been mentioned. Dickens wrote in 1853 that 'in a utilitarian age, of all other times, it is a matter of grave importance that fairy tales should be respected.' Some of the fairy

Colour Plate 78. **ARTHUR CLAUDE STRACHAN.** A Devon Cottage

painters worked in watercolour, in particular John Anster Fitzgerald (Plate 39). The Doyle brothers, Richard (known as Dicky) and Charles Altamont, worked mainly in watercolour, and both painted fairy and fantasy subjects (Colour Plate 79 and Plate 40). Many other artists illustrated children's books and fairy tales, such as the talented amateur Eleanor Vere Boyle, who signed herself 'EVB'. The wife of a Somerset rector, she illustrated a number of children's books, of which the best known is *The Story Without an End.* Her illustrations, done in watercolour and then chromo-lithographed, are small, brightly coloured and full of whimsical fantasy (Plate 41). Watercolour is the ideal medium for exploring the surreal world of fairy tales.

The Aesthetic Movement also embraced those second-generation Pre-Raphaelites of the 1870s who exhibited at the Dudley and the Grosvenor. Their presiding deity was Burne-Jones, and like him they favoured romantic literary and historical subjects, often with a strongly Italianate flavour. Evelyn De Morgan, J.R. Spencer Stanhope, Walter Crane (Plate 42) and Robert Bateman all fall into this category, and have been mentioned earlier. They all used watercolours, though heavily mixed with bodycolour in the Burne-Jones manner. Walter Crane in his *Reminiscences* of 1907 summarised what they all felt about Burne-Jones's watercolours of the 1860s: 'The curtain has been lifted, and we had a glimpse into a magic world of romance and pictured poetry, peopled with ghosts of "ladies dead and lovely knights" – a twilight world of dark mysterious woodlands, haunted streams, meads of deep green starred with burning flowers, veiled in a dim and mystic light . . .' This is the intensely romantic dream world that these artists were trying to re-create.

Colour Plate 79. **RICHARD DOYLE.** The Fairies' Dance

Plate 40. **CHARLES ALTAMONT DOYLE.** A Moon Fantasy

Plate 41. **ELEANOR VERE BOYLE.** The Spirits of Fair Love

Plate 42. **WALTER CRANE.** Near Bettws-y-Coed, North Wales

Plate 43. **EDWARD JOHN POYNTER.**
Music Heavenly Maid

Plate 44. **GEORGE LAWRENCE BULLEID.**
Binding the Fillet

Another artist who exhibited at the Grosvenor was Albert Joseph Moore. Although his pictures are outwardly classical, Moore was a passionate colourist and aesthete, and during the 1860s a close friend of Whistler. Moore worked mainly in oil, but did occasionally produce watercolours which are characterised by the same formality of design and delicate subtlety of colour as is found in his oils. The poise, beauty and clarity of his watercolours, combined with a deliberate absence of historical or mythological reference, makes them some of the purest and most beautiful expressions of the Aesthetic Movement (Colour Plate 80).

Among the other classicists, Leighton, Watts and Waterhouse did not make more than occasional use of watercolour. Alma-Tadema and Poynter, however, were both talented watercolourists. Alma-Tadema used the watercolour to make repeat versions of his oils, as did another Grosvenor Gallery artist, Tissot. But in his later years, Alma-Tadema began to produce separate watercolours of classical figures which display the same dazzling brilliance as his oils. Usually small and with only a few figures (unlike the Roman spectaculars of his paintings), they are simply celebrations of light, colour and surface, rendered with all his extraordinary dexterity (Colour Plate 81). Alma-Tadema had many imitators, but few rivals. Among his better followers in watercolour were Henry Ryland, George Lawrence Bulleid (Plate 44) and William Anstey Dollond.

Another classicist to make frequent use of watercolour was Edward John Poynter (Plate 43). As a young man, in the 1860s and 1870s, he frequently used watercolour for portrait commissions. These were mostly of rich and artistic ladies, such as Lady Elcho, one of the leaders of The Souls, a group of aristocratic friends who cultivated

Colour Plate 80. **ALBERT JOSEPH MOORE.** A Yellow Room

a deliberately artistic and intellectual approach to life. In these watercolours, Poynter displays a refinement that is typical of the Aesthetic Movement. The sitter, her dress, the room and the objects are all carefully arranged so as to create a harmonious and satisfying composition. Walter Crane also painted portraits of artistic ladies in artistic interiors, often in watercolour. This was a genre attempted by many artists at the time (Plate 45), especially those who exhibited at the Dudley and the Grosvenor. Edward Clifford, a follower of Burne-Jones, produced many beautiful portraits in watercolour or pastel, usually female heads or half-lengths, with floral backgrounds of sunflowers or lilies, two of the favourite flowers of the aesthetes. The most skilled practitioner of this genre was Frederick Sandys. His portraits in coloured chalks are some of the most astonishing technical feats ever achieved in this difficult medium.

As we have already seen, the Aesthetic Movement had a considerable influence on landscape painting. Most aesthetic painters of landscape preferred to include figures, in the Birket Foster or Helen Allingham manner. Only a few remained faithful to pure landscape, such as J.W. North and Albert Goodwin. Another group to concentrate on landscape painting were the Etruscans, a group of English artists who worked in Italy, especially in the Roman Campagna. They were all much influenced by the Italian Giovanni Costa, a close friend of Lord Leighton, and believed above all that the painting of landscape had to be enhanced by poetic feeling and imagination. Mere recording of facts was not enough. Costa believed in first making studies from nature, on the spot, and then working them up into finished works in the studio. This was the traditional method of landscape painting, but was diametrically opposed to the Pre-Raphaelite philosophy of painting a picture entirely outdoors. Only a few of the Etruscans worked in watercolour, including Matthew Ridley Corbet and George Howard, 9th Earl of Carlisle.

The Aesthetic Movement continued to influence watercolour painting for the rest of the

Colour Plate 81. **LAWRENCE ALMA-TADEMA.** A Priestess of Apollo

century, and in the personality of an artist like Albert Goodwin, it survived well into the twentieth century. The movement dramatically changed the course of watercolour painting in England. It greatly increased the range of subjects; it pushed the use of new techniques and materials to their limits; and it focused artists' attention once again on the need for beauty, imagination and feeling in painting, rather than the mere recording of facts. The Ruskinian landscape had become the aesthetic landscape. Mid-Victorian morality had been replaced by the cult of beauty.

Plate 45.
GUSTAVUS ARTHUR BOUVIER.
In the Morning

159

Plate 46. **WALLER HUGH PATON.** Anglers near Dollar, Scotland

Plate 47. **WILMOT PILSBURY.** Evington Brook

Plate 48. **JOSEPH KIRKPATRICK.** The Gentle Art

Later Victorian Watercolourists

The career of a Victorian watercolourist could hardly be better summed up than by the life and work Albert Goodwin. As we have seen, as a young man, he had been a pupil of the Pre-Raphaelites, in particular Arthur Hughes and Ford Madox Brown. They introduced him to Ruskin, who was to be an important influence, particularly in encouraging Goodwin to emulate Turner, and in 1872, Ruskin took Goodwin with him on a trip to Italy. Goodwin's earliest works were in oil, and throughout his life, he continued to paint oils occasionally. His earlier watercolours are strongly Pre-Raphaelite in style, with bright clear colours and plenty of attention to detail. But gradually he began to develop his own unique style, a combination of Pre-Raphaelite, aesthetic and Turneresque elements.

Goodwin was to become one of the most widely-travelled of all Victorian artists, visiting most of Europe, as well as Egypt, India, the South Sea Islands and the West Indies. He remained a loyal supporter of the RWS, becoming a member in 1881. He explored the possibilities of the watercolour medium to its limits, making constant use of bodycolour, sponging and stippling and often working over pen and ink. Goodwin knew all the technical tricks of the watercolour trade, but as he moved away from Pre-Raphaelitism, his style became progressively more atmospheric and misty. He especially delighted in effects of sunset and twilight and few watercolorists have painted them better (Colour Plate 82). Although a painter of places, his prime concern was to convey a sense of romance and poetry. He was a romantic topographer, in the tradition of Turner, and the spirit of place was to him more important than mere reality. Goodwin also absorbed many of the ideas of the Aesthetic Movement, not only in his strongly romantic approach, but in his use of surprising and unusual viewpoints, and his habit of leaving much of the composition empty. In his many watercolours of the Alps, for example, he loved to pick out the peaks of the mountains, illuminated by the sun, while everything in the valleys

Colour Plate 82. **ALBERT GOODWIN.** The Citadel, Cairo

below was still dark and indistinct. Some of his watercolours in the Himalayas veer off into complete fantasy, with weird temples set against improbable backgrounds of craggy mountains wreathed in mist. Pictures like these would make perfect illustrations for the novels of Rider Haggard. But in the main, Goodwin remained rooted in topography, in the spirit of place. His work is among the finest romantic topography of the nineteenth century, and he was Turner's only real successor.

The late Victorian period produced a huge crop of landscape watercolourists (Plate 46), so it is only possible to mention a few of the better ones. Many of these were from the provinces, or worked in a particular area. Wilmot Pilsbury, for example, was based for most of his life in Leicester, where he was head of the local school of art. He was an RWS member and regular exhibitor there. His landscape and country scenes were painted with great delicacy and sensitivity, and his work was compared to Helen Allingham's, for it exudes a genuine love of English landscape and the picturesque hamlets of the Midlands (Plate 47).

Liverpool was a prolific breeding ground for artists of all kinds, watercolourists included. Many of them studied under the Liverpool watercolourist John Finnie, who was head of the local Mechanics' Institute and School of Art. One of his pupils was Joseph Kirkpatrick who painted delightful watercolours of country scenes. These are usually idyllic celebrations of English summer, with plenty of meadows and girls in white bonnets (Plate 48). This was a formula repeated by many a Victorian watercolourist, often with sugary results, but in the hands of an artist like Kirkpatrick it was carried out with sufficient delicacy and restraint to avoid this pitfall. Another Liverpool watercolourist was David Woodlock, who developed a very distinctive impressionist style. He painted country scenes and village life, usually involving ancient half-timbered cottages. He also worked in Venice and it

Colour Plate 83. **THOMAS McKAY.** In the Garden

Colour Plate 84. **JOHN ATKINSON.** Tynemouth Sands, Northumberland

Plate 49. **DAVID WOODLOCK.** The Piazza San Marco, Venice

was here that he painted many of his best works (Plate 49).

Thomas McKay was another watercolourist working in the Liverpool area. Very little is known of his career, and until recently there was even confusion about his Christian name, and he was for a time known as John or James McKay. He too developed a distinctive and delicately impressionistic style. Once seen, his moody landscapes and country scenes have a recognisable flavour of their own, displaying a penchant for pink and purplish colours, especially when trying to capture the effects of evening light (Colour Plate 83). Another talented northerner was John Atkinson of Newcastle, whose robustly impressionist watercolours are remarkably similar to the early work of Alfred Munnings. Like Munnings, Atkinson enjoyed painting horse fairs, gypsy camps, meets of the hounds, and donkeys on the beach. He worked in Northumberland, Durham and North Yorkshire and his watercolours present us with a marvellously lively and spirited picture of country life in the north-east at that period (Colour Plate 84).

The most popular county for artists in the Victorian period was Surrey (Plate 50). It was still at that time remarkably unspoiled, offering both beautiful scenery and picturesque villages. It also had the advantage of the railway, which offered speedy transport to the centre of London. Both Birket Foster and Helen Allingham lived there, and literally hundreds of other artists either settled or visited in the summer. A watercolourist particularly associated with Surrey was Sutton Palmer, painter of many idyllic views of that county as well as of the River Wye, and who illustrated one of the A. & C. Black books on Surrey. George Marks lived in Kent, but he too painted the landscape of Surrey as well as that of Sussex. His watercolours are generally

Plate 50. **JAMES WALSHAM BALDOCK.** A Surrey Lane

Colour Plate 85. **JOHN WHITE.** A Cornfield

Colour Plate 86. **BENJAMIN WALTER SPIERS.** 'Armour, Prints, Pictures, Prints, China
(all crack'd), Old Rickety Tables and Chairs Broken – Back'd'

Colour Plate 87. **THOMAS JAMES LLOYD.** An Evening I Remember

pleasing and idyllic, but at times they can have a more mysterious mood, especially when he introduced rather threatening flocks of crows into them. Another artist who painted in the region, this time in Kent and Sussex, was Thomas James Lloyd. He too painted idyllic, pastoral scenes, sometimes on quite a large scale, as well as highly romantic watercolours of gardens (Colour Plate 87).

John White is associated with the West Country. Many of his landscapes were painted near the Devon coast, and at their best these have a highly idyllic quality, especially those involving harvest fields (Colour Plate 85). He also painted village scenes, both in Devon and the south-east. Altogether different was the work of William Fraser Garden, an obscure provincial who spent his whole life in the fens near St. Ives, Huntingdon. His remarkable watercolour landscapes of the fen country with its slow streams, willow trees and timbered buildings, are quite exceptional in their detail,

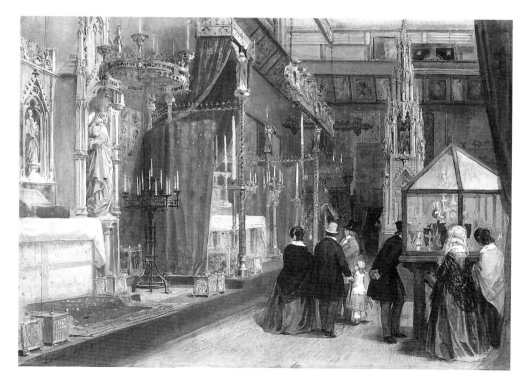

Plate 51.
LOUIS HAGHE.
Interior of the Medieval
Court, Great Exhibition

167

Plate 52. **WILLIAM FRASER GARDEN.** The Old Mill, Hemingford Grey, St. Ives

Plate 53. **THOMAS ALLOM.** Osborne House, Isle of Wight

168

Colour Plate 88. **GEORGE SAMUEL ELGOOD.** Barncluith, Lanarkshire

clarity and stillness (Plate 52). Garden worked entirely for local patrons, and until recently his work was quite unknown outside the area. His real name was William Garden Fraser, but he rearranged his names in order to distinguish himself from his numerous brothers. He certainly was the most remarkable artist of the Fraser family.

As well as landscape, marine and coastal scenes were also popular subjects for Victorian watercolourists. Many of the marine painters already mentioned also worked in watercolour, for example Clarkson Stanfield, E.W. Cooke and George Chambers. Some artists, such as John Henry Mole, and two West Country artists, John and Thomas Mogford, spent almost their entire careers painting coastal scenes. Both Charles Napier Hemy and Montague Dawson used watercolours. So did the two royal marine artists, J.C. Schetky and Oswald Brierley. Several watercolourists worked almost entirely for the royal family, recording state ceremonies, royal events and travels (Plates 51 and 53). These artists included Willliam Simpson, who also worked in the Crimea, Robert Taylor Prichett and George Henry Thomas. Carl Haag produced many delightful watercolours of Queen Victoria, Albert and their children on holiday at Balmoral. Haag also painted scenes of Arab life in the tradition of J. F. Lewis and Frederick Gooodall, and it is for those watercolours that he is better known for today.

Gardens and Flowers

Watercolour is a medium particularly well suited to the painting of gardens (Plate 54), and Victorian artists produced countless watercolours of gardens and flowers. There was even a small school of artists who specialised only in these subjects all their lives, and I have written at length about this school in the book entitled *Painted Gardens*. Interest in gardening and garden history increased during the Victorian

Plate 54. **FREDERICK HAMILTON JACKSON.** In the Garden

Plate 55. **EDWARD KINGTON BRICE.** Border with Poppies

Plate 56. **THOMAS HUNN.** The Orangery at Mount Edgecumbe, Devon

period, and a school of garden painters emerged primarily to satisfy a demand from the proud owners of gardens to have them recorded. Furthermore, illustrations were needed to fill the many books and periodicals about gardening that proliferated in the late nineteenth century. The three main artists of this school were George Samuel Elgood, Ernest Arthur Rowe and Beatrice Parsons.

Undoubtedly, the greatest of the garden artists was Elgood. A professional watercolourist, and member of the RI, he was not only a highly accomplished watercolourist, but also extremely knowledgeable about gardens, plants and garden design. He travelled to Italy almost every year, painting gardens, eventually producing a book, *Italian Gardens* (1907), which he also illustrated. His knowledge and love of Italian gardens gave him a strong sense of the importance of structure and design in a garden, and in most of his watercolours Elgood always emphasises architectural features, such as balustrades and terraces, flights of steps, fountains, old walls and statuary. He also loved clipped yew hedges and topiary and no English artist has painted them better (Colour Plate 88).

Elgood's most famous book, *Some English Gardens*, was published in 1904, with the commentaries on each garden by Gertrude Jekyll. Here one can see his work at its best. His preference was for old and historic gardens such as Levens, Melbourne, Penshurst, Cleeve Prior and Montacute, and these were to inspire many of his finest works. When he came to paint flowers, Elgood also showed a finely developed sense of colour. He painted many herbaceous borders and flower gardens, always using soft pale colours, bathed in a wonderfully subtle, blue-green haze. He fully understood Jekyll's premise that the art of gardening was the art of painting pictures, in other words, the crucial skill of controlling colour combinations and gradations. Elgood held no less than twelve one-man exhibitions at the Fine Art Society before

Colour Plate 89. **ERNEST ARTHUR ROWE.** Bulwick, Northamptonshire

the First World War. His output was greater than any other garden painter, except possibly that of Beatrice Parsons, and his work represents a fascinating historical record of the famous and interesting gardens of the late nineteenth century, many of which have since disappeared or been drastically altered.

Elgood's only rival was Ernest Arthur Rowe, who also lived in Kent, and who also spent much of his time painting in Italy. Elgood and Rowe painted many of the same gardens, sometimes from the same spot. Rowe's style tends to be somewhat brighter and harder than Elgood's, but some of his large views of gardens such as Arley, Berkeley Castle, Penshurst or Bulwick (Colour Plate 89), are as fine as anything by Elgood. Rowe's diaries and notebooks are still in the possession of his family, and so we know a great deal about his life and work. His notebooks reveal how difficult it was for a garden watercolourist to make a living. Between 1885 and 1895 he earned about £100 a year and in 1890 only £30. By 1900, his earnings had risen to about £300, and he felt able to marry.No wonder so many Victorian watercolourists turned to oil painting.

The work of Beatrice Parsons, the third of the triumvirate of garden artists, is very different from that of Elgood or Rowe. Instead of formal gardens full of topiary and architectural elements, Parsons liked above all to paint borders and flower gardens in the full glory of their summer colours. In *Painted Gardens* I christened her 'the queen of the blazing border.' Her work evokes the world of the Victorian and Edwardian flower garden and exudes a wonderful feeling of heat and sunshine. It also tells us a great deal about how borders were planted, for Parsons was brilliantly clever at delineating flowers (Colour Plate 90), and excelled at painting spring gardens, especially in the West Country, with trees in blossom and spring bulbs in

Colour Plate 90. **BEATRICE PARSONS.** Rock Garden and Columbines, Sedgwick Park, Sussex

bloom. She also painted rhododendron and azalea gardens, usually in Cornwall. Her many clients and admirers included Queen Mary, William Robinson of Gravetye Manor, and Lord Battersea. She painted gardens all over the south of England, and was commissioned to record gardens in the south of France and North Africa. She worked on into the 1920s and 1930s, but gradually the demand for her type of work faded away. The idyllic world of the great Edwardian garden had gone forever, and Beatrice Parsons died, completely forgotten in 1955.

Apart from the professional garden painters, there were a number of landscape painters who occasionally included gardens in their repertoire. One such was Alfred Parsons (no relation to Beatrice. Parsons) who lived in Broadway where he built a house and laid out his own garden, and where he also designed several other gardens. His watercolours of gardens are painted with a strong sense of design (Colour Plate 92). Parsons' main claim to fame nowadays are his illustrations to *The Genus Rosa*, a *magnum opus* conceived and paid for by a redoubtable spinster Miss Ellen Willmott, one of the great gardeners of the day. To illustrate it, Parsons produced 132 watercolours. The book was finally published in 1914, after a quarrel between Parsons, Miss Willmott and the publishers, John Murray.

Another watercolourist who seems to have made a regular speciality of gardens was Thomas Hunn. He lived near Guildford, and mostly painted gardens in Surrey, such as Clandon, Great Tangley and Sutton Place. Hunn had a pale, delicate style, which is quite distinctive and his watercolours of gardens have considerable subtlety (Plate 56). Other lesser known practitioners include Henry M. Terry, L.N.

Nottage and the two Tyndales, Walter and Thomas (Plate 58). Walter Tyndale was a much-travelled topographer illustrating books on Japan, Egypt and Italy. Two other landscapists who occasionally painted gardens are Ernest Albert Chadwick and Edward Kington Brice (Plate 55). Both were capable of producing outstandingly attractive garden scenes, and one can only wish they had done more of them. Both Thomas James Lloyd (Colour Plate 87) and Edward Killingworth Johnson painted large and showy watercolours of gardens, but usually as a setting for figures.

Painting gardens and flowers were among the favourite pastimes of the Victorian lady. Some lady amateurs attained a professional standard and exhibited their work in public. One such was the remarkable Irish watercolourist, Mildred Anne Butler, who became an associate of the RWS. She painted both landscapes and gardens in Ireland in a delightfully fluid and impressionistic style. Another extremely talented lady was Margaret Waterfield, who came to garden painting by way of illustration. Between 1905 and 1922 she illustrated a number of gardening books, in a style that

Plate 57. **MARY E. DUFFIELD.** Roses

Plate 58. **THOMAS TYNDALE.** Gorcott Hall, near Redditch, Worcestershire

Colour Plate 91. **LILIAN STANNARD.** Summer Borders

is surprisingly broad and impressionistic, and yet which manages to convey the shapes and colours of the flowers extremely well.

The most productive of the lady garden painters were the two Stannards, Lilian and Theresa Sylvester, members of the Bedfordshire family of Stannards, one of those remarkable artistic dynasties of the Victorian period. Lilian's brother, Henry John Sylvester Stannard, was best known for his watercolours of picturesque village scenes, and occasionally watercolours of gardens. His daughter, Theresa Stannard, and her aunt, Lilian, became specialists in garden subjects. Both the Stannards developed a distinctly bright, impressionistic style in which the flowers are not delineated with the same precision as those of Beatrice Parsons. Nor are their gardens usually identifiable, but with titles like 'Summer Borders' or 'A Sunny Corner' they are meant to be evocations of English gardens in summer, rather than representations of specific places (Colour Plate 91). Both the Stannards also painted cottage gardens, the domain of Helen Allingham and Birket Foster. Conversely, although Allingham is most famous for her watercolours of cottages, it should not be forgotten that she also depicted formal gardens, in particular Gertrude Jekyll's garden, Munstead Wood, and Lord Tennyson's gardens at Farringford on the Isle of Wight, and at Aldworth in Surrey.

Large numbers of lady artists painted watercolours of flowers and still-life. Space only permits mention of a few of these, such as Mary Duffield (Plate 57), the wife

Colour Plate 92. **ALFRED WILLIAM PARSONS.** China Roses, Broadway

Plate 59. **MARIAN CHASE.** Cowslips and Orchids

of the still-life painter William Duffield. Ladies of artistic families often took to flower painting, such as Marian Chase (Plate 59), daughter of the watercolourist John Chase. Another such was Helen Cordelia Coleman, the sister of William Stephen Coleman. Augusta Withers painted fruit, flowers and birds in a boldly-coloured, slightly primitive style, and her watercolours are avidly collected and appreciated today. All these ladies, and numerous others, carried the painting of flowers and fruit in watercolour to an extremely high level of finish and delicacy.

Lady Artists
Watercolour was considered the domain of lady artists in the Victorian period. Proficiency in watercolours was regarded as an accomplishment among the middle and upper classes, and among these two classes enormous numbers of ladies practised the art of watercolour painting (for example Plates 60 and 61). Many were no more than talented amateurs; some acquired semi-professional status; many became full-time professionals. As we have seen, Helen Allingham and Kate Greenaway became both well-known and successful artists. It is worth considering, therefore, the work of some other notable lady watercolorists.

Ladies of the aristocracy were allowed to exhibit their work in public, but it was not considered appropriate to sell them. Lady Waterford, for example, was a highly talented watercolourist, whose work was admired by Ruskin, Burne-Jones and Watts (Plate 62). She held exhibitions of her work, and occasionally showed at the Grosvenor Gallery, but very rarely sold anything. Mostly she gave her watercolours

Plate 60. **W. GEORGINA CUNNINGHAM.** The White Shell

to friends or relatives. Her main memorial is the series of biblical scenes of children which she painted on the walls of the village school at Ford, Northumberland. As we have seen, Eleanor Vere Boyle was a talented watercolourist and children's book illustrator. Married to a son of the Earl of Cork, she did sell her works for use as illustrations, but used the initials 'EVB' to conceal her identity.

Ladies belonging to the county gentry, however, seemed to have no qualms about selling their work and many of them did so. Mildred Anne Butler, the Irish watercolourist, has already been mentioned as a painter of gardens. She also painted landscapes, animals and country scenes and exhibited them at the Royal Academy and the RWS. Another Irish lady artist was Rose Barton, chiefly known for her exceptionally delicate and atmospheric watercolours of London. She exhibited her work widely, at the Academy and the Grosvenor, as well as at the RWS, of which she was elected a full member in 1911.

Pre-Raphaelite circles also included a number of women artists, some of them relations, others friends and pupils. Barbara Bodichon was a friend of Rossetti, who often stayed at her house in Sussex, and described her as 'blessed with large rations of tin, fat, enthusiasm and gold hair.' She married a French doctor and travelled extensively, painting watercolour landscapes and views wherever she went. Some

Colour Plate 93. **MARY L. GOW.** An Invitation

Colour Plate 94. **MARIE SPARTALI.** La Pensierosa

of her larger landscapes are impressive essays in the Pre-Raphaelite manner. She was also something of a pioneer feminist, and one of the founders of Girton College, Cambridge.

Another disciple of Rossetti, although a pupil of Madox Brown, was Marie Spartali, now generally known under her married name of Marie Stillman. Born of Greek parents living in London, Spartali was considered a beauty and often modelled for Rossetti, Burne-Jones and the photographer Julia Margaret Cameron. Her own pictures are generally of female heads or half-length figures in watercolour, and very much in the Rossetti vein (Colour Plate 94). Ford Madox Brown's daughters, Catherine and Lucy, were also watercolourists, who painted figurative subjects in the Pre-Raphaelite manner. Lucy was married to Rossetti's

Plate 61. **ISABEL NAFTEL.** Winifred Mary Bombass, aged 10

Plate 62. **LOUISA, LADY WATERFORD.**
The Infant Jesus: 'He was Subject unto Them'

brother, William Michael. Rosa Brett, the sister of John, painted small watercolour studies of landscape that are remarkable for their clarity and precision.

Another sister of an artist was Mary Gow, whose brother was the historical painter Andrew Carrick Gow. She married another painter, Sydney Prior Hall, but continued to paint under her maiden name, using both oil and watercolour to produce some delightful pictures of children, especially young girls. These paintings tread that uncertain territory between sentimental and sentimentality, yet always somehow strike just the right balance (Colour Plate 93). At their best, Mary Gow's pictures are some of the most delightful studies of Victorian childhood. Two sisters, Adelaide and Florence Claxton, the daughters of the historical painter Marshall Claxton, also painted watercolours of children, often featuring a ghost or apparition (Plate 63). Their works are sometimes humorous and often have a strongly moral twist.

The painting of interiors was another area in which ladies tended to excel. Victorian ladies spent much of their time at home and therefore had the time to record every aspect of domestic life. Many who did so were amateurs, but one whose work was of higher than average standard was Mary Ellen Best. Her remarkable interiors of houses in her native York have only relatively recently come to light, but are now justly admired and sought after by collectors. She later married a German teacher and went to live in Germany, where she painted many more

Plate 63. **ADELAIDE CLAXTON.** Wonderland

delightful interiors, especially of china cabinets and rooms in museums.

Artistic families were a feature of the Victorian age. The Hayllars have already been mentioned, as have the prolific Stannards of Bedfordshire. Another dynasty was that of the Rayners. Samuel Rayner, an architectural painter and watercolourist, had no less than five daughters and one son, all of them artists. The most celebrated of these today is Louise Rayner. She specialised in detailed but lively watercolours of the streets and market places of historic towns, such as Salisbury, Ludlow and Chester, and now much prized for their topographical accuracy (Plate 64). Many of the wives of Victorian artists were also painters, often following their husband's style and

Plate 64. **LOUISE RAYNER.** Old Hastings

Plate 65.
EDGAR BUNDY.
Sisters

184

Colour Plate 95. **CHARLES GREEN.** Her First Bouquet

subject matter. Henrietta Ward, the wife of Edward Matthew Ward the historical painter, was also the daughter of a painter, George Raphael Ward. Elizabeth Stanhope Forbes, wife of the Newlyn painter, Stanhope Forbes, was another. She painted mainly in oil, but also produced delightful watercolours and pastels. Her subjects were very similar to those of her husband – fisherfolk and country life in Cornwall.

Later Figurative Watercolourists

The tradition of painting narrative scenes and interiors with figures continued to the end of the century and beyond (for example Plates 65-72). Typical of those painting this type of watercolour was Charles Green. Like so many others of his generation, he first worked as a black and white illustrator, mainly for *Once a Week*. He then turned to watercolour, and became a member of the RI. Like Birket Foster, he used bright colours, enhanced by bodycolour, and a stippling technique. He preferred interiors to landscapes, usually with figures, and liked rooms with plenty of clutter. He had illustrated Dickens, and 'Little Nell in the Old Curiosity Shop' was one of his favourite subjects. Some of his large and elaborate works, such as 'Her First Bouquet', are among the finest of Victorian narrative watercolours (Colour Plate 95). Green died in 1898.

Another typical late Victorian figure was George Goodwin Kilburne. Although he did sometimes paint in oil, most of his work was in watercolour, and he joined the RI in 1866. He produced many delightful scenes of Victorian life, indoors (Plate 74), in gardens and set in landscapes. Like many others, he also catered for that almost limitless Victorian appetite for scenes in eighteenth century or Regency dress. Kilburne went on producing these well into the twentieth century, dying in

Plate 66.
THOMAS FALCON MARSHALL.
Christmas Morning

Plate 67.
EDWARD RADFORD.
A Lady asleep in a Chair

Plate 68. **CHARLES JAMES ADAMS.** An Artist's Son

1924. The work of his son, George Goodwin Kilburne, Junior, who died in 1938, is confusingly similar to that of the father, the main difference being that Kilburne junior signed his name in capital letters.

Very few Victorian watercolourists painted realist scenes of working-class life. This was mainly left to the oil painters, for example Luke Fildes, Frank Holl and Hubert von Herkomer. One exception was John Henry Henshall. His oil painting 'The Public Bar' is one of the best Victorian realist pictures, fit to stand comparison with Courbet, Gustave Doré, or the French school. Henshall also produced a watercolour version of it, now in the London Museum. His other watercolours are mostly interiors with figures, usually displaying a delicate sense of colour combined with a sensibility typical of the Aesthetic Movement. Edward Frederick Brewtnall's glorious watercolour 'Where Next?' transports us far away from the gritty realities of Victorian urban life. Here we see a handsome and well-dressed Victorian couple,

Plate 69. **RALPH HEDLEY.** The Sleeping Model

presumably on their honeymoon, poring over a map on a sunny terrace somewhere by the Mediterranean. This enchanting watercolour is typical of the many surprises that can be found in later Victorian narrative painting (Colour Plate 96).

The cottage idyll was a genre to which the Victorians were inordinately attached, and many watercolourists made a speciality of this subject. One prolific practitioner was Carlton Alfred Smith. His cottage interiors are always meticulously observed and usually contain one female figure, modelled from his wife, who looks suspiciously pretty and well-dressed to find herself in such a humble cottage (Plate 73). This is typical of the way in which Victorian narrative painters fused reality with fantasy. They studied objects in detail to give authenticity to their pictures, as if attention to detail in small matters licensed evasion in larger ones. Thus Carlton Smith's cottage interiors may look realistic, but they give a misleadingly cosy picture of what a Victorian cottage probably looked like. Nevertheless, they are always beautifully rendered, and doubtless found ready buyers. Smith went on repeating this successful formula well into the twentieth century, dying in 1946. Another artist with a penchant for depicting cottage interiors, often with an elderly Darby and Joan couple, was Henry Spernon Tozer, who was working from 1900 to

Colour Plate 96. **EDWARD FREDERICK BREWTNALL.** Where Next?

Plate 70. **JOSEPH MIDDLETON JOPLING.** Three Friends

Plate 71. **FREDERICK SMALLFIELD.** Town Mice

1930. Although a twentieth century artist, Tozer's work is completely Victorian in spirit, rather like that of another Victorian survivor, Charles Spencelayh.

The fisherman's cottage was another favourite subject to which watercolourists were attracted. Many of the artists who gathered at the favoured seaside resorts, such as Cullercoats in Northumberland and Staithes in Yorkshire, painted in watercolour as well as in oil. Robert Jobling of Newcastle, for example, used watercolour for many of his scenes of fishing life. He painted both at Staithes and at Cullercoats, where the American artist Winslow Homer was a visitor in the 1880s. Many of the Newlyn artists occasionally used watercolour, in particular Walter Langley and Ralph Todd, both of whom concentrated on depicting the daily life and work of fisherfolk.

Plate 73. **CARLTON ALFRED SMITH.** A Stitch in Time

Plate 74. **GEORGE GOODWIN KILBURNE.** Demeter: In the British Museum

Colour Plate 97. **JAMES ABBOTT McNEILL WHISTLER.** Chelsea

Impressionism

In the late 1880s, more and more artists began to study on the Continent, especially in Holland and France. Inevitably these continental influences began to have their effect on English art. At the same time the debate as to the relative merits of oil and watercolour had subsided, and by the end of the century oil and watercolour were both regarded as valid mediums.

French Impressionism exerted a powerful influence over many English artists, watercolourists included, but there were other influences at work. The career of George Clausen is typical of many a late Victorian artist. As a young man he studied at the Antwerp Academy, and his early work reflects the influence of the Hague School, especially Anton Mauve and the Maris Brothers. Most of his early watercolours are studies of fisherfolk and boats, and they combine the restrained colouring, casual composition and atmospheric effects typical of the Hague School. Later, however, Clausen moved towards a much brighter, more impressionist style, which clearly shows French influence. In 1886, he was one of the founders of the New English Art Club, dedicated to spreading the influence of French Impressionism. For the rest of his career, Clausen painted mainly in oil, but he continued to use watercolour and pastel, often to work out ideas and compositions for his oils. His subjects, as always, were agricultural labourers (Colour Plate 98). Although he became an Impressionist in technique, he never lost his strong sense of form and composition.

Whistler began to use watercolour in the 1880s, thus bringing the medium into the forefront of aesthetic debate. He had lived in Paris and was familiar with the French Impressionists, but he also admired the delicacy and restraint of Japanese art, and was an admirer of the late work of Turner, still at that time largely unknown and misunderstood. In 1884, at the Dowdeswell Gallery in London, he exhibited a group

Colour Plate 98. **GEORGE CLAUSEN.** The Mowers

of watercolours for the first time. Most of his watercolours are small, and at first glance, slight. They require closer inspection to appreciate the full subtlety of their delicate overlapping washes of pure colour. Whistler believed that his watercolours should be suggestive and atmospheric, rather than state the obvious, leaving the imagination of the viewer to do the rest (Colour Plate 97).

Whistler was one of the chief propagandists of the Aesthetic Movement. In his celebrated *Ten O'Clock Lecture* in 1885, he stated that 'Nature contains the elements, in colour and form, of all pictures, as the keyboard contains the notes of all music. But the artist is born to pick and choose, and group with science, these elements, that the result may be beautiful.' Whistler was a perfectionist, and went to great lengths to make his pictures appear spontaneous and natural. In other words, all trace of labour and finish must be eliminated. This is the paradox of the Aesthetic Movement, and one which exercised the minds and faculties of many Victorian watercolourists.

Whistler's aesthetic doctrines were a little too extreme and audacious for most people, but he nonetheless had many admirers and followers. Mortimer Menpes

Plate 75. **MORTIMER MENPES.** Outside a Japanese Tea House

was his pupil and his watercolours show distinct Whistlerian influence, especially his shopfronts and street scenes (Plate 75). Menpes travelled widely, painting in India and Japan, and many of his watercolours were used as illustrations for travel books, particularly those published by A. & C. Black. The development of coloured book illustrations, together with improvements in printing, greatly contributed to establishing watercolour as a serious medium.

Two other watercolourists whose work shows Whistler's influence are Albert Ludovici, Junior, and the grandiloquently named Hercules Brabazon Brabazon. Ludovici fell under Whistler's spell during the latter's brief and turbulent period as President of the RBA (Royal Society of British Artists). His watercolours are generally London street scenes, especially in Piccadilly and Hyde Park (Colour Plate 99), painted in a delicate and stylish impressionist style that certainly owes something to Whistler, although his subjects are more reminiscent of French painters of the boulevards, such as Jean Beraud. Brabazon studied watercolour and travelled together with Ruskin and Arthur Severn. A founder member of the New English Art Club in 1886, he had intended to remain an amateur, but in 1892 his friend John Singer Sargent persuaded him to hold an exhibition at the Goupil Gallery. The show was an immediate success, and Brabazon's watercolours have

Plate 76. **ARTHUR MELVILLE.** An Islamic Court

remained popular with collectors ever since. His style is broad and rapid, and pushes the technique of the Impressionist watercolour to its limits (Colour Plate 101). Although his work owes much to the example of Whistler, as well as Turner, it is closest to the watercolour style of his mentor and friend, Sargent.

The lessons of Whistler and French impressionism were better appreciated in Scotland than in England. The late nineteenth century was a flourishing period of art in Scotland and saw the founding of the so-called Glasgow Boys. Like many such associations, this was a loose and fluctuating group of like-minded young

Colour Plate 99. **ALBERT LUDOVICI.** Rotten Row, Hyde Park Corner

Colour Plate 100.
JOSEPH CRAWHALL.
A Cockerel

Colour Plate 101. **HERCULES BRABAZON BRABAZON.** A Church in Venice

artists, rather than a coherent school. But much of the brightest talent of the day belonged to the Glasgow School, as it is called, even if for only a short period. Many of the painters were watercolourists, and space only permits mention of a few of them. Arthur Melville might stand as a typical example. After studying in Paris and travelling in the Middle East, he returned to Scotland by 1884, where he quickly became part of the Glasgow School. By 1889 he had been elected an RWS, and then settled in London. He developed a brilliantly rapid impressionistic style, quite distinctively his own, and continued to find inspiration in the Middle East and North Africa, attracted by the vivid colours and the light, both of which suited his style (Plate 76).

Another artist in Glasgow during those fruitful 1880s was Sir John Lavery. He had studied in London and Paris, and was already developing his own impressionist style. During these early years he often used watercolour, usually as a study or preparation for an oil. Like many artists of this period, Lavery found watercolour an ideal medium for experimenting, both with colour and with composition, and some of his watercolour studies are more daring and more striking, than the finished oils.

One of the most brilliant of the Glasgow artists, and one to make extensive use of watercolour, was Joseph Crawhall. He worked on silk or linen to get the spontaneous effects he wanted for his favourite subjects – horses, dogs and birds, especially ducks. His style is particularly delicate and subtle in its luminosity and colouring, and has often been compared to Chinese art (Colour Plate 100).Crawhall set great value on rapidity of execution and immediacy of effect, and perhaps no watercolourist attained such dexterity in achieving it. He would finish parts of his watercolours more completely than others, leaving some areas blank or thinly covered with a transparent wash. William Burrell, the great collector and shipbuilder, was a fervent admirer of his work, and a large group of Crawhall's works can be seen at the Burrell Collection in Glasgow. Crawhall was working around the turn of the century, and died in 1913. It is fitting therefore to end this survey with him, one of the most brilliant exponents of the art of watercolour.

Details of Illustrations in

Victorian Painting

(Measurements are height by width, metric measurements to the nearest .5cm)

Frontispiece. Eleanor Fortescue-Brickdale. 'They toil not neither do they spin'. Signed with initials and dated 1903. Watercolour. 16 x 10½ins. (40.5 x 26.5cm). Christopher Wood Gallery, London

Colour Plates (Oil)

Colour Plate l. (p.9) George Clausen. Harvest — Tying the Sheaves. Signed and dated 1902. 33 x 25ins. (84 x 63.5cm). Richard Green

Colour Plate 2. (p.13) John Atkinson Grimshaw. October Gold. Signed and dated 1889. 23½ x 17½ins. (59.5 x 44.5cm). Christopher Wood Gallery, London

Colour Plate 3. (p.16) Richard Dadd. Contradiction — Oberon and Titania. Signed and dated 1854-1858. Oval, 24 x 29¾ins. (61 x 75.5cm). Private Collection

Colour Plate 4. (p.17) Richard Redgrave. The Emigrants' Last Sight of Home. Signed and dated 1858. 27 x 39ins. (68.5 x 99cm). The Tate Gallery, London

Colour Plate 5. (p.20) William Powell Frith. Many Happy Returns of the Day (sketch). Oil on board. 11¾ x 15¾ins. (30 x 40cm). York City Art Gallery

Colour Plate 6. (p.20) George Elgar Hicks. The General Post Office at One Minute to Six. Signed and dated 1860. 35 x 53ins. (89 x 134.5cm). Museum of London

Colour Plate 7. (p.21) William Holman Hunt. The Hireling Shepherd. Signed and dated 1851. 30 x 43ins. (76 x 109cm). Manchester City Art Gallery

Colour Plate 8. (p.24) Ford Madox Brown. Work. Signed and dated 1852-1865. Arched top. 53 x 77ins. (134.5 x 195.5cm). Manchester City Art Gallery

Colour Plate 9. (p.25) Arthur Hughes. April Love. Signed and dated 1855-1856. Arched top.35 x 19½ins. (89 x 49.5cm). The Tate Gallery, London

Colour Plate 10. (p.28) William Dyce. Pegwell Bay. 24½ x 34½ins. (62 x 87.5cm). The Tate Gallery, London

Colour Plate 11. (p.29) John Brett. The Val d'Aosta. Signed and dated 1858. 34½ x 26⅞ins. (87.5 x 68cm). Private Collection

Colour Plate 12. (p.32) Dante Gabriel Charles Rossetti. Beata Beatrix. Signed with monogram and dated 1864-1870. 34 x 26ins. (86.5 x 66cm). The Tate Gallery, London

Colour Plate 13. (p.35) John Everett Millais. Mariana. Signed and dated 1851. 23½ x 19½ins. (59.5 x 49.5cm). The Makins Collection

Colour Plate 14. (p.39) Sir Edward Burne-Jones. Study for the Sleeping Princess in the Briar Rose series. Gouache, 38 x 58ins. (96.5 x 147cm). Sotheby's

Colour Plate 15. (p.43) Anthony Frederick Augustus Sandys. Queen Eleanor. Signed with monogram and dated 1858. 16 x 12ins. (40.5 x 30.5cm). The National Museum of Wales

Colour Plate 16. (p.47) John William Waterhouse. Pandora. Signed and dated 1896. 60 x 36ins. (152.5 x 91.5cm). Private Collection

Colour Plate 17. (p.49) Frederic, Lord Leighton. Invocation. 55 x 33ins. (139.5 x 84cm). Private Collection

Colour Plate 18. (p.52) Daniel Maclise. King Cophetua and the Beggar Maid. 48 x 72ins. (122 x 183cm). Courtesy of the Prudential Assurance Company PLC

Colour Plate 19. (p.53) George Frederic Watts. Hope. 59 x 43ins. (150 x 109cm). Private Collection

Colour Plate 20. (p.57) Lawrence Alma-Tadema. The Colosseum. Signed and dated 1896. Oil on panel. 44 x 29ins. (111.5 x 73.5cm). Private Collection

Colour Plate 21. (p.60) John William Godward. Absence Makes the Heart Grow Fonder. Signed and dated 1912. 50 x 31ins. (127 x 78.5cm). Photograph: Christopher Wood Gallery, London

Colour Plate 22. (p.61) Edward John Poynter. A Roman Boat Race (1889). 24 x 18ins. (61 x 45.5cm). Photograph: Sotheby's

Colour Plate 23. (p.64) Albert Joseph Moore. A Revery. 46 x 29½ins. (117 x 75cm). Private Collection. Photograph: Agnew's, London

Colour Plate 24. (p.66) Sidney Harold Meteyard. Venus and Adonis. 41½ x 43½ins. (105.5 x 110.5cm). Private Collection. Photograph: Christopher Wood Gallery, London

Colour Plate 25. (p.67) Hubert von Herkomer. Hard Times. Signed with initials and dated '85. 33½ x 43½ins. (85 x 110.5cm). Manchester City Art Gallery

Colour Plate 26. (p.67) Frank Holl. Deserted. Signed and dated 1874. 36¼ x 53½ins. (92 x 136cm). Photograph: Christopher Wood Gallery, London

Colour Plate 27. (p.70) James Hayllar. Ready for the Party. Signed and dated 1866. 35 x 27½ins. (89 x 70cm). Private Collection

Colour Plate 28. (p.71) James Tissot. The Captain and the Mate. Signed and dated '73. 21 x 30ins. (53.5 x 76cm). Private Collection

Colour Plate 29. (p.74) John Singer Sargent. Carnation Lily Lily Rose. 68½ x 60½ins. (174 x 153.5cm). The Tate Gallery, London

Colour Plate 30. (p.75) James Abbott McNeill Whistler. The Little White Girl: Symphony in White, No. 2. Signed. 30 x 20 ins. (76 x 51cm). The Tate Gallery, London

Colour Plate 31. (p.78) Benjamin Williams Leader. An Old Manor House by a Stream. Signed and dated 1871. 19¼ x 26ins. (49 x 66cm). Richard Green Gallery, London

Colour Plate 32. (p.79) George Vicat Cole. The Hop Gardens. Signed and dated 1862. 24 x 36ins. (61 x 91.5cm). Richard Green Gallery, London

Colour Plate 33. (p.82) Thomas Sidney Cooper. Canterbury Meadows. Signed and dated 1858. 30 x 45ins. (76 x 114.5cm). Richard Green Gallery, London

Colour Plate 34. (p.82) John Linnell. Wheat. Signed and dated 1860. 39 x 53ins. (99 x 134.5cm). Photograph: Sotheby's

Colour Plate 35. (p.83) Samuel Luke Fildes. The Village Wedding. Signed and dated 1883. 60 x 100ins. (152.5 x 254cm). Private Collection

Colour Plate 36. (p.86) Henry Herbert La Thangue. A Sussex Orchard. Signed. 36 x 41ins. (91.5 x 104cm). Richard Green Gallery, London

Colour Plate 37. (p.87) William H. Snape. Cottage Interior. Signed and dated 1891. 14 x 18ins. (35.5 x 45.5cm). Private Collection

Colour Plate 38. (p.90) George Earl. King's Cross — Going North. Signed and dated 1893. 48½ x 84ins. (123 x 213.5cm). The Railway Museum, York

Colour Plate 39. (p.91) Edwin Henry Landseer. Scene in Braemar — Highland Deer. 106½ x 106½ins. (270.5 x 270.5cm). Private Collection

Colour Plate 40. (p.94) Edward William Cooke. Dutch Trawlers at Anchor, Scheveningen. Signed and dated 1863. 36¼ x 54½ins. (92 x 138.5cm). Martyn Gregory Gallery, London

Colour Plate 41. (p.95) George Chambers, Jnr. The Thames at Greenwich. Signed and dated '67. 33½ x 57ins. (85 x 146cm). Richard Green Gallery, London

Colour Plate 42. (p.97) Henry Nelson O'Neil. Before Waterloo. Signed and dated 1868. 72 x 55ins. (183 x 139.5cm). Private Collection

Colour Plate 43. (p.100) David Roberts. Philae, Egypt. Signed and dated 1843. 30½ x 60½ins. (77.5 x 153.5cm). Fine Art Society, London

Colour Plate 44. (p.101) John Frederick Lewis. The Midday Meal, Cairo. Signed and dated 1875. 34½ x 45½ins. (87.5 x 115.5cm). Private Collection

Colour Plate 45. (p.101) Edward Lear. Corfu. Signed with monogram and dated 1859. 27½ x 45½ins. (70 x 115.5cm). Christopher Wood Gallery, London

Colour Plate 46. (p.104) Stanhope Alexander Forbes. The Health of the Bride. Signed and dated 1889. 60 x 78¾ins. (152.5 x 200cm). The Tate Gallery, London

Colour Plates (Watercolour)

Colour Plate 47. (p.105) Sir John Gilbert, RA. The Field of the Cloth of Gold. Signed with monogram and dated 1862. 19 x 26ins. (48 x 66cm).Christopher Wood Gallery, London.

Colour Plate 48. (p.109) Joseph Mallord William Turner, RA. The Entrance to the Grand Canal. 8½ x 12½ins. (21.5 x 31.5cm). Sotheby's

Colour Plate 49. (p.109) Joseph Mallord William Turner, RA. Florence. 13⅞ x 20½ins. (35 x 52cm). Agnew's

Colour Plate 50. (p.112) Thomas Miles Richardson, Jnr. Cowhill Fair, Newcastle. Signed and dated 1835. 8¾ x 12½ins. (22 x 31.5cm). Christopher Wood Gallery, London

Colour Plate 51. (p.113) David Cox. Haddon Hall, Derbyshire. Signed. 7 x 9¼ins. (17.5 x 23cm). Agnew's

Colour Plate 52. (p.116) Samuel Palmer. Illustration to Milton's *Lycidas*. Indistinctly signed. 15½ x 23ins. (39 x 58cm). Agnew's

Colour Plate 53. (p.117) William Henry Hunt. Bird's Nest and Blossom. Signed. 9 x 12½ins. (22.5 x 31.5cm). Sotheby's

Colour Plate 54. (p.117) John Sherrin. Bird's Nest and Blossom. Signed. 8⅞ x 10⅜ins. (22.5 x 26cm). Christopher Wood Gallery, London

Colour Plate 55. (p.120) William Hough. Apples and Grapes. Signed. 7 x 10½ins. (17.5 x 26.5cm). Christopher Wood Gallery, London

Colour Plate 56. (p.121) William Henry Hunt. Interior of a Barn. 21¾ x 30ins. (55 x 76cm). Sotheby's

Colour Plate 57. (p.121) John Frederick Lewis. A Halt in the Desert. Signed and dated 1856. 14½ x 19½ins. (36.5 x 49.5cm). Sotheby's

Colour Plate 58. (p.122) Ford Madox Brown. Elijah and the Widow's Son. Signed with monogram and dated 1864. 15½ x 10ins. (39 x 25cm). Sotheby's

Colour Plate 59. (p.123) William Holman Hunt. A Wadi in Palestine. Signed, inscribed and dated September. 13¼ x 19¼ins. (33.5 x 48.5cm). Sotheby's

Colour Plate 60. (p.125) Dante Gabriel Rossetti. Lady Lilith. Signed with monogram and dated 1867. 21½ x 17ins. (54.5 x 43cm). Sotheby's

Colour Plate 61. (p.127) Sir Edward Burne-Jones. The Annunciation. 23¾ x 20¾ins. (60 x 52.5cm). Private Collection

Colour Plate 62. (p.129) Sir Edward Burne-Jones. Sunset and Corn. Signed with initials. 10 x 7½ins. (25 x 19cm). Christopher Wood Gallery, London

Colour Plate 63. (p.130) John Roddam Spencer-Stanhope. The Washing Place. 26¾ x 47½ins. (67.5 x 120.5cm). Sotheby's

Colour Plate 64. (p.131) Evelyn de Morgan. Hero. Signed with monogram and dated 1885. 22¾ x 11½ins. (57.5 x 29cm). Sotheby's

Colour Plate 65. (p.132) Simeon Solomon. Shadrach, Meshak and Abednego in the Fiery Furnace. Signed with monogram and dated 10.63. 16 x 10½ins. (40.5 x 26.5cm). Christopher Wood Gallery, London

Colour Plate 66. (p.133) John Byam Shaw. Diana of the Hunt. Signed and dated 1901. 29 x 20½ins. (73.5 x 52cm). Sotheby's

Colour Plate 67. (p.135) John Ruskin. Baden, Switzerland. Signed with initials. 9 x 7⅛ins. (22.5 x 18cm). Christopher Wood Gallery, London

Colour Plate 68. (p.136) George Price Boyce. Streatley Mill at Sunset. 15½ x 20ins. (39 x 50.5cm). The Robertson Collection, Orkney

Colour Plate 69. (p.138) Albert Goodwin. A Mountain Stream. Signed and dated '84. 13¾ x 20½ins. (34.5 x 52cm). Chris Beetles Ltd, London

Colour Plate 70. (p.138) Myles Birket Foster. The Itinerant Fiddler. Signed with monogram. 11¾ x 17½ins. (29.5 x 44cm). Sotheby's

Colour Plate 71. (p.139) Richard Redgrave. Parkhurst Woods, Abinger, Surrey. 10 x 15ins. (25 x 38cm). Victoria and Albert Museum/Photo Bridgeman Library

Colour Plate 72. (p.142) George Shalders. The Shepherd Boy. 19 x 31¾ins. (48 x 80.5cm). Christopher Wood Gallery, London

Colour Plate 73. (p.143) Edmund George Warren. Lost in the Woods. Signed and dated 1859. 28 x 18½ins. (71 x 46.5cm). Christopher Wood Gallery, London

Colour Plate 74. (p.146) Myles Birket Foster. Boys Fishing from a Punt. Signed with monogram. 13¾ x 23½ins. (34.5 x 59.5cm). Polak Gallery, London/Photo: Sotheby's

Colour Plate 75. (p.147) Frederick Walker. Strange Faces. 24 x 31ins. (60.5 x 78.5cm). Photo: Fine Art Society, London

Colour Plate 76. (p.150) Kate Greenaway. Through the White Flowers. Signed and dated 1891. 14 x 21ins. (35.5 x 53cm). Chris Beetles Ltd, London

Colour Plate 77. (p.151) Helen Allingham. Cottage at Brook, near Witley, Surrey. Signed. 11 x 7ins. (27.5 x 17.5cm). Christopher Wood Gallery.

Colour Plate 78. (p.154) Arthur Claude Strachan. A Devon Cottage. Signed. Christopher Wood Gallery, London

Colour Plate 79. (p.155) Richard Doyle. The Fairies' Dance. Signed and dated 1875. 10¼ x 17½ins. (26 x 44cm). Sotheby's

Colour Plate 80. (p.158) Albert Joseph Moore. A Yellow Room. Signed with anthemion. 16 x 6ins. (40.5 x 15cm). Sotheby's

Colour Plate 81. (p.159) Sir Lawrence Alma-Tadema, RA. A Priestess of Apollo. Signed and inscribed. 5 x 12ins. (12.5 x 30cm). Sotheby's

Colour Plate 82. (p.162) Albert Goodwin. The Citadel, Cairo. Signed, inscribed and dated 1928. 13 x 19ins. (33 x 48cm). Christopher Wood Gallery, London

Colour Plate 83. (p.163) Thomas McKay. In the Garden. Signed and dated 1912. 6 x 8¾ins. (15 x 22cm). Christopher Wood Gallery, London

Colour Plate 84. (p.163) John Atkinson. Tynemouth Sands, Northumberland. Signed and dated '08. 9¾ x 13¾ins. (24.5 x 34.5cm). Private Collection/Photo: Christopher Wood Gallery, London

Colour Plate 85. (p.166) John White. A Cornfield. Signed. 10 x 13½ins. (25 x 34cm). Christopher Wood Gallery, London

Colour Plate 86. (p.166) Benjamin Walter Spiers. 'Armour, Prints, Pictures, Prints, China (all crack'd), Old Rickety Tables and Chairs Broken – Back'd'. Signed. 27 x 48ins. (68.5 x 121.5cm). Christopher Wood Gallery, London

Colour Plate 87. (p.167) Thomas James Lloyd. 'An Evening I Remember'. Signed and dated 1897. 18 x 44ins. (45.5 x 111.5cm). Christopher Wood Gallery, London

Colour Plate 88. (p.169) George Samuel Elgood. Barncluith, Lanarkshire. Signed and dated 1900. 13¾ x 19⅞ins. (34.5 x 50cm). Christopher Wood Gallery, London

Colour Plate 89. (p.172) Ernest Arthur Rowe. Bulwick, Northamptonshire. Signed and dated 1898. 19½ x 29ins. (49.5 x 73.5cm). Christopher Wood Gallery, London

Colour Plate 90. (p.173) Beatrice Parsons. Rock Garden and Columbines, Sedgwick Park, Sussex. Signed. 10 x 14ins. (25 x 35.5cm). Christopher Wood Gallery, London

Colour Plate 91. (p.176) Lilian Stannard. Summer Borders. Signed. 20 x 32½ins. (50.5 x 82.5cm). Christopher Wood Gallery, London

Colour Plate 92. (p.177) Alfred Parsons. China Roses, Broadway. Signed. Christopher Wood Gallery, London

Colour Plate 93. (p.180) Mary Gow. An Invitation. Signed with initials and dated 1881. 18¼ x 12¾ins. (46 x 32cm). Christopher Wood Gallery, London

Colour Plate 94. (p.181) Marie Spartali (Mrs Stillman). La Pensierosa. Signed with monogram and dated '79. 21¼ x 17½ins. (53.5 x 44cm). Christopher Wood Gallery, London

Colour Plate 95. (p.185) Charles Green. Her First Bouquet. 21½ x 31ins. (54.5 x 78.5cm). Chris Beetles Ltd, London

Colour Plate 96. (p.189) Edward Frederick Brewtnall. Where Next? 18½ x 28¾ins. (46.5 x 73cm). Christopher Wood Gallery, London

Colour Plate 97. (p.192) James Abbott McNeill Whistler. Chelsea. 5 x 8½ins. (12.5 x 21.5cm). Sotheby's

Colour Plate 98. (p.193) Sir George Clausen, RA. The Mowers. Signed and dated 1885. 12½ x 14ins. (31.5 x 35.5cm). Sotheby's

Colour Plate 99. (p.196) Albert Ludovici. Rotten Row, Hyde Park Corner. Signed. 10 x 15ins. (25 x 38cm). Christopher Wood Gallery, London.

Colour Plate 100. (p.196) Joseph Crawhall. A Cockerel. Signed. 17½ x 23ins. (44 x 58cm). Sotheby's

Colour Plate 101. (p.197) Hercules Brabazon Brabazon. A Church in Venice. Signed. 4¼ x 7¼ins. (10.5 x 18cm). Chris Beetles Ltd, London

Black and White Plates (Oil)

Plate 1. (p.14) George Richmond. John Ruskin. (c.1843). Chalks. 17 x 14ins. (43 x 35.6cm). National Portrait Gallery, London

Plate 2. (p.15) William Powell Frith. Claude Duval. Signed. 30¾ x 43ins. (78 x 109cm). Photograph: Sotheby's

Plate 3. (p.23) Dante Gabriel Charles Rossetti. Study of Jane Morris. Dated 26 July 1870. Pencil. 12½ x16½ins. (32 x 42cm). Christopher Wood Gallery, London

Plate 4. (p.27) Henry Wallis. The Stonebreaker. Signed and dated 1857. Oil on panel. 25¾ x 31ins. (65.5 x 78.5cm). Birmingham City Museum and Art Gallery

Plate 5. (p.31) William Bell Scott. The Gloaming — a Manse Garden in Berwickshire. Signed and dated 1862. 13 x 19ins. (33 x 48.5cm). Formerly McCormick Collection. Photograph: Christopher Wood Gallery, London

Plate 6. (p.41) Edward Coley Burne-Jones. The Mirror of Venus. Etching after Burne-Jones by Felix Jasinski. 13¼ x 21ins. (33.5 x 53.5cm). Christopher Wood Gallery, London

Plate 7. (p.59) Edward John Poynter. The Catapult. Signed with monogram and dated 1868-1872. 61 x 72½ins. (155 x 184cm). Laing Art Gallery, Newcastle upon Tyne

Plate 8. (p.63) Albert Joseph Moore. A Musician. Signed with anthemion device. 10½ x 15ins. (26.5 x 38cm). Mellon Centre for British Art, Yale, USA

Plate 9. (p.85) George Elgar Hicks. Asleep in the Cornfield. 11 x 13ins. (28 x 33cm). Private Collection

Plate 10. (p.88) George Samuel Elgood. The Gardens at Melbourne Hall, Derbyshire. Signed and dated 1894. 9¼ x 14ins. (23.5 x 35.5cm). Photograph: Christopher Wood Gallery, London

Plate 11. (p.89) George Lance. Still-life. Signed and dated 1855. 44½ x 56ins. (113 x 142cm). Photograph: Christie's

Plate 12. (p.96) Ernest Crofts. From Quatre Bras to Waterloo. Signed and dated 1881. 22¼ x 41½ins. (56.5 x 105cm). Photograph: Sotheby's

Black and White Plates (Watercolour)

Plate 13. (p.107) Edward Henry Corbould. After Dinner. Signed and dated 1890. 23½ x 18½ins. (59.5 x 46.5cm). Christopher Wood Gallery, London

Plate 14. (p.108) James Duffield Harding. Lyon from the River. 9 x 13ins. (22.5 x 33cm). Sotheby's

Plate 15. (p.108) Samuel Prout. L'Hotel de Ville, Brussells. Signed and dated 1842. 26½ x 35ins. (67 x 88.5cm). Sotheby's

Plate 16. (p.111) William Lake Price. The Interior of a Gothic Chapel. Signed and dated 1837. 21 x 24½ins. (53 x 61.5cm). Christopher Wood Gallery, London

Plate 17. (p.113) William Callow. View from the Terrace at Versailles. 11½ x 17¾ins. (29 x 45cm). Sotheby's

Plate 18. (p.114) Anthony Vandyke Copley Fielding. Shoreham, Kent. Signed and dated 1839. 11½ x 15¾ins. (29 x 40cm). Agnew's

Plate 19. (p.115) David Roberts, RA. Christian and Mohammedan Churches on the Summit of Mount Sinai. Inscribed and dated Feb. 20, 1839. 10 x 13¾ins. (25 x 34.5cm). Christopher Wood Gallery, London

Plate 20. (p.118) William Leighton Leitch. On Lake Maggiore. Signed and dated 1866. 23¼ x 36½ins. (59 x 92.5cm). Sotheby's

Plate 21. (p.119) Joseph Nash. The Drawing Room, Ashton Hall, Warwickshire. Signed. 12½ x 18¼ins. (31.5 x 46cm). Sotheby's

Plate 22. (p.120) Augustus Osborne Lamplough. An Arab Warrior on a Camel in the Desert. Signed. 20¾ x 35½ins. (52.5 x 90cm). Christopher Wood Gallery, London

Plate 23. (p.124) John Riley Wilmer. The Virgin and Child. Signed and dated 1913. 27 x 14ins. (68.5 x 35.5cm). Christopher Wood Gallery, London

Plate 24. (p.126) Henry Meynell Rheam. 'Once upon a Time'. Signed. 31 x 17ins. (78.5 x 43cm). Christopher Wood Gallery, London

Plate 25. (p.128) Henry John Stock. The Poet's Dream. Signed and dated 1881. 18 x 21ins. (45.5 x 53cm). Christopher Wood Gallery, London

Plate 26. (p.129) Thomas Matthew Rooke. A Lych Gate. 11¼ x 20ins. (28.5 x 50cm). Peter Nahum Ltd, London

Plate 27. (p.134) William Bell Scott. Hexham Market Place, Northumberland. 19 x 23ins. (48 x 58cm). Sotheby's

Plate 28. (p.134) John Brett. The Castle of Joree. 5 x 6¾ins. (12.5 x 17cm). Sotheby's

Plate 29. (p.137) John William Inchbold. Greenwich, London. 14 x 20½ins. (35.5 x 52cm). Sotheby's

Plate 30. (p.140) Alfred William Hunt. Time and Tide. 23¾ x 35½ins. (60 x 90cm). Sotheby's

Plate 31. (p.141) William Henry Millais. Woodland Steps. 12¼ x 9ins. (31 x 22.5cm). Sotheby's

Plate 32. (p.142) John George Sowerby. Flowers by a Rocky Stream. Signed. 5½ x 10½ins. (13.5 x 26.5cm). Christopher Wood Gallery, London

Plate 33. (p.144) Arthur Severn. Old Hungerford Bridge, Chelsea. 7½ x 11½ins. (19 x 29cm). Christopher Wood Gallery, London

Plate 34. (p.145) John William North. A Woodland Spring. 17 x 11½ins. (43 x 29cm). Chris Beetles Ltd, London/Photo: Sotheby's

Plate 35. (p.148) George John Pinwell. The Pied Piper of Hamelin. Signed. 11¼ x 21ins. (29.5 x 53cm). Sotheby's

Plate 36. (p.149) Robert Walker MacBeth. A Summer's Day by the Millpond. Signed and dated 1899. 12½ x 19ins. (31.5 x 48cm). Sotheby's

Plate 37. (p.149) Sir Hubert von Herkomer. A Weary Way. Signed and dated '91. 10 x 14ins. (25 x 35.5cm). Sotheby's

Plate 38. (p.152) Charles Edward Wilson. A Difficult Problem. Signed. 12½ x 8½ins. (31.5 x 21.5cm). Christopher Wood Gallery, London

Plate 39. (p.153) John Anster Fitzgerald. The Fairy Falconer. Signed with initials. 7 x 8ins. (17.5 x 20cm). Christopher Wood Gallery, London

Plate 40. (p.155) Charles Altamont Doyle. A Moon Fantasy. 9¾ x 15¼ins. (24.5 x 38.5cm). Maas Gallery, London

Plate 41. (p.156) Eleanor Vere Boyle. The Spirits of Fair Love. 7 x 10¼ins. (17.5 x 26cm). Sotheby's

Plate 42. (p.156) Walter Crane. Near Bettws-y-Coed, North Wales. Signed. 8¼ x 12¼ins. (20.5 x 31cm). Christopher Wood Gallery, London

Plate 43. (p.157) Sir Edward John Poynter, PRA. Music Heavenly Maid. 19 x 13ins. (48 x 33cm). Sotheby's

Plate 44. (p.157) George Lawrence Bulleid. Binding the Fillet. Signed and dated MCMVII. 19 x 13¼ins. (48 x 33.5cm). Christopher Wood Gallery, London

Plate 45. (p.158) Gustavus Arthur Bouvier. In the Morning. Signed and dated 1877. 13½ x 16¾ins. (34 x 42.5cm). Christopher Wood Gallery, London

Plate 46. (p.160) Waller Hugh Paton. Anglers near Dollar, Scotland. Signed and dated 1874. Christopher Wood Gallery, London

Plate 47. (p.160) Wilmot Pilsbury. Evington Brook. Signed and dated 1885. 10¼ x 14½ins. (26 x 36.5cm). Sotheby's

Plate 48. (p.161) Joseph Kirkpatrick. The Gentle Art. Signed and dated 1898. 20 x 31ins. (50 x 78.5cm). Christopher Wood Gallery, London

Plate 49. (p.164) David Woodlock. The Piazza San Marco, Venice. Signed and dated 1894. 9 x 13½ins. (22.5 x 34cm). Christopher Wood Gallery, London

Plate 50. (p.165) James Walsham Baldock. A Surrey Lane   Signed. 5½ x 12ins. (13.5 x 30cm). Christopher Wood Gallery, London

Plate 51. (p.167) Louis Haghe. Interior of the Medieval Court, Great Exhibition. Signed. 12½ x 15½ins. (31.5 x 39cm). Christopher Wood Gallery, London

Plate 52. (p.168) William Fraser Garden. The Old Mill, Hemingford Grey, St. Ives. Signed and dated 1889. 13 x 18ins. (33 x 45.5cm). Christopher Wood Gallery, London

Plate 53. (p.168) Thomas Allom. Osborne House, Isle of Wight. 8½ x 15½ins. (21.5 x 39cm). Christopher Wood Gallery, London

Plate 54. (p.170) Frederick Hamilton Jackson. In the Garden. Signed and dated 1894. 14 x 21ins. (35.5 x 53cm). Christopher Wood Gallery, London

Plate 55. (p.170) Edward Kington Brice. Border with Poppies. Signed. 15½ x 22¼ins. (39 x 56.5cm). Christopher Wood Gallery, London

Plate 56. (p.171) Thomas Hunn. The Orangery at Mount Edgecumbe, Devon. Signed and dated '03. 13¼ x 19½ins. (33.5 x 49.5cm). Christopher Wood Gallery, London

Plate 57. (p.174) Mary E. Duffield. Roses. Signed. 14½ x 21½ins. (36.5 x 54.5cm). Christopher Wood Gallery, London

Plate 58. (p.175) Thomas Tyndale. Gorcott Hall, nr. Redditch, Worcs. 10½ x 7½ins. (26.5 x 19cm). Christopher Wood Gallery, London

Plate 59. (p.178) Marian Chase. Cowslips and Orchids. Signed. 11½ x 16ins. (29 x 40.5cm). Christopher Wood Gallery, London

Plate 60. (p.179) W. Georgina Cunningham. The White Shell. Signed with monogram. 13 x 16ins. (33 x 40.5cm). Christopher Wood Gallery, London

Plate 61. (p.182) Isabel Naftel. Winifred Mary Bombass, aged 10. Signed and dated 1872. 18 x 12½ins. (45.5 x 31.5cm). Christopher Wood Gallery, London

Plate 62. (p.182) Lady Waterford. The Infant Jesus: 'He was Subject unto Them'. 7⅞ x 4¾ins. (19.5 x 12cm). Christopher Wood Gallery, London

Plate 63. (p.183) Adelaide Claxton. Wonderland. Signed on reverse. 23½ x 20½ins. (59.5 x 52cm). Christopher Wood Gallery, London

Plate 64. (p.184) Louise Rayner. Old Hastings. Signed. 14¾ x 21¼ins. (37 x 53.5cm). Sotheby's

Plate 65. (p.184) Edgar Bundy. Sisters. Signed and dated 1896. 11 x 14ins. (27.5 x 35.5cm). Christopher Wood Gallery, London

Plate 66. (p.186) Thomas Falcon Marshall. Christmas Morning. Signed with initials and dated 1865. 15¾ x 23½ins. (40 x 59.5cm). Christopher Wood Gallery, London

Plate 67. (p.186) Edward Radford. A Lady asleep in a Chair. Signed. 10½ x 12ins. (26.5 x 30cm). Christopher Wood Gallery, London

Plate 68. (p.187) Charles James Adams. An Artist's Son. Signed and dated 1882. 9¾ x 8½ins. (24.5 x 21.5cm). Christopher Wood Gallery, London

Plate 69. (p.188) Ralph Hedley. The Sleeping Model. Signed and dated 1888. 23 x 18ins. (58 x 45.5cm). Christopher Wood Gallery, London

Plate 70. (p.189) Joseph Middleton Jopling. Three Friends. Signed and dated 1865. Christopher Wood Gallery, London

Plate 71. (p.189) Frederick Smallfield. Town Mice. Signed. 17¼ x 12½ins. (43.4 x 31.5cm). Christopher Wood Gallery, London

Plate 72. (p.190) John Simmons. A Young Girl by a Stream. 20¼ x 14½ins. (51 x 36.5cm). Christopher Wood Gallery, London

Plate 73. (p.191) Carlton Alfred Smith. A Stitch in Time. Signed and dated 1902. 19 x 27½ins. (48 x 69.5cm). Sotheby's

Plate 74. (p.191) George Goodwin Kilburne. Demeter: In the British Museum. Signed. 6 x 9ins. (15 x 22.5cm). Christopher Wood Gallery, London

Plate 75. (p.194) Mortimer Menpes. Outside a Japanese Tea House. 12½ x 15¾ins. (31.5 x 40cm). Sotheby's

Plate 76. (195) Arthur Melville. An Islamic Court. 21 x 15ins. (53 x 38cm). Sotheby's